Testament

TESTAMENT

GEORGE L. GOODWIN

RESOURCE *Publications* · Eugene, Oregon

TESTAMENT

Resource Publications
An Imprint of Wipf and Stock Publishers
199 W. 8th Ave., Suite 3
Eugene, OR 97401

www.wipfandstock.com

PAPERBACK ISBN: 978-1-6667-5391-2
HARDCOVER ISBN: 978-1-6667-5392-9
EBOOK ISBN: 978-1-6667-5393-6

09/28/22

Contents

1

Prelude

THIS IS A RECORD of the most important things I have learned in my life. It is not intended as a scholarly or technical treatise, although it may seem too scholarly for some and not scholarly enough for others. I am writing less for academic specialists than for generalists, intellectually curious people who are interested in the topics I am considering.

What I have to say reflects my life experiences—as a father, a husband, a seminarian, a soldier, a teacher, a dean, a college president, and most of all, as a student of theology. I am indebted to the thinkers who have most influenced me—especially theologians Schubert Ogden and Reinhold Niebuhr, philosophers Alfred North Whitehead and Charles Hartshorne, and colleagues Philip Devenish, Tom West and Will Mowchan. I've been fortunate to have the freedom—in the sense of having my basic needs met—to reflect. It's hard to think about big things when you are hungry or scared.

Living reflectively is not easy. It takes considerable effort to try to understand one's life, to make sense of the adventure. I believe that we should learn from our labors and that we ought to pass along what we have learned. Our ancestors learned by trial and error which plants were healthy to eat, and which were poisonous, and their descendants benefitted from their lessons. Why not the same with life as a whole? As we reach our later years, we ought to reflect on our major life lessons and share them, especially with the young. It is an act of accountability and of responsibility. People ask me if I have drawn up a will so that my physical and financial estate will be passed on, but no one ever asks what lessons I want to leave for others. This is my intellectual will.

There are, of course, many important things that one learns in life—about success and failure, effort and reward, disappointment and disillusionment, friendship and love, and so much more. But the most important thing to learn is what our lives *mean*. In the words of the modern composer Gustav Mahler, "Wherefore hast thou lived? Wherefore hast thou suffered? Is it all some great, fearful joke?"[1]

THE EXISTENTIAL QUESTION

Albert Camus begins one of his essays dramatically: "There is but one truly serious philosophical problem, and that is suicide. Judging whether life is or is not worth living amounts to answering the fundamental question of philosophy."[2] This declaration goes right to the heart of the matter: Does life have a point, and, if so, what is it?

This question about the meaning of human life is what I want to address. I will call it *the existential question*.

I am not saying that we are always consciously considering Camus' philosophical challenge or mulling Mahler's questions. Most of us do not wake up each day asking what our lives mean. A lot of our time is taken up with practical issues and with various pursuits that, in fact, distract us from thinking about the bigger questions; for example, just trying to make ends meet in poorer communities, and conspicuous consumption and the denial of death in wealthy communities.

But there are hints that the existential question is at work just below the surface. Examples include:

- Yearning, the longing for homecoming. Plato wrote that the human soul existed before its bodily incarnation, and that

1. Nussbaum quoting Mahler, *Upheavals of Thought*, 620.
2. Camus, *The Myth of Sisyphus and Other Essays*, 3.

during our lives we long to return to the eternal realm. St. Augustine wrote that our hearts are made for God, and they are restless until they rest in God.

- The desire to make a difference. Alfred North Whitehead said that one of the fundamental human desires is that our lives are more than "passing whiffs of insignificance." Irish novelist and playwright Samuel Beckett talked about leaving "a stain upon the silence."[3] We want to be part of a larger whole, to contribute to something greater than ourselves, something that endures.

- The sense of lost innocence, of the gap between what we could be and what we are; the longing for forgiveness and redemption.

The existential question is inevitable; it cannot lie dormant or be suppressed indefinitely, and it erupts into our consciousness on noteworthy occasions, such as:

- The funeral of a loved one;

- An act of violence that seems senseless and indiscriminate;

- A moment of extreme boredom, tedium or ennui;

- A period of profound guilt or loneliness or despair, when we want to be rescued from ourselves;

- The celebration of a birth or a wedding, or any of the other "peak experiences" of human life.

At such times we find ourselves face to face with the question: What is this all about? What do our lives mean? We might even define a human being as the being who asks what it means to be a human being.

Answering this question is also unavoidable. Even if someone says "I'm not interested in that abstract question of what life means, I've got more important practical matters to attend to"—even then we have a proposed answer: A human being is a being that is uninterested in what it is. There is simply no ultimate dodge on this question.

3. Bair, *Samuel Beckett*, 640.

We answer the question of life's meaning by how we live. Unlike the objects and events we experience—a chair, a football game, a sonnet—there is no pre-set definition of what being human means. We each paint our own portrait and put it on public display: *This* is what it means to be human! Unlike other animals who simply live their lives without reflecting on them, we lead our lives as well as live them. We create ourselves. We define who we are by how we live. As one thinker put it: our existence determines our essence.

How we answer the existential question is important. It not only determines how we understand ourselves; it also provides the Rosetta Stone in terms of which we interpret everything else. To give one example: At the moment, our country is engaged in a vigorous debate about multiculturalism and national identity. Underlying the struggle over immigration, diversity, and "America first" is a question about life's meaning: Is it best understood as a struggle between competing interests, where the strong survive and might makes right, or is human life more a matter of cooperation, partnership, and empathy? This is not a "mere" intellectual discussion. The answers to these questions reflect how we understand ourselves as human beings. Ideas matter.

POTENTIAL ANSWERS

There are three possible answers to the existential question: Life has no meaning; life has proximate meaning only; or life has final meaning. In Western thought, these three answers correspond to the positions of nihilism, atheistic humanism, and theism.

1. Nihilism says that life is meaningless; the existential question is either meaningless, or it expresses a wish that cannot be fulfilled. In Macbeth's memorable formulation: "Life is a tale told by an idiot, full of sound and fury, signifying nothing." Or, as another thinker would have it, "the entire history of our species is like breath on cold window panes." There, and quickly gone. Life doesn't *mean* anything. It just is, and then it isn't. Kafka says that "the meaning of life is that it ends."

2. Atheism says that life has no final meaning, but it does have proximate or intermediate meaning. Life ends at death, but it is not therefore absurd. Life has whatever meaning we can (and should) find or create here and now for each other and bequeath to our children and to society. Atheistic philosophers like Bertrand Russell and Jean-Paul Sartre were political activists and social reformers. They represent a kind of heroic humanistic atheism. But in the end, as Russell says, "we are simply curious accidents in a backwater."

3. Theism says that life does have a final meaning that survives our death, the inevitable death of our species, and even the death of nature as we know it. There is some transcendent point to existence. This conviction is reflected in various teachings such as reincarnation or the immortality of the soul or the resurrection of the body.

We also may call the existential question *the religious question*. Calling the question "religious" is not a thinly-disguised attempt to pre-load its answer. Rather, I am drawing on the fact that religion is the major form of human culture that attempts to raise and answer the question of life's meaning. In the words of theologian Paul Tillich, religion deals with matters of ultimate concern in human life. Religions provide ultimate contexts, encompassing frames of reference, within which we understand our lives and everything else. This reaching for an explanatory frame of reference I will call the religious impulse or the religious dimension in human life. In Reinhold Niebuhr's words: "All forms of religious faith are principles of interpretation which we use to organize our experience."[4]

It is important to distinguish between the religious *dimension* or the religious *impulse* in human life and *religions*. Organized religions are expressions of the religious impulse, rather than vice versa. That is to say, organized religions rise out of the human search for meaning; they are the major way we humans give structural expression to the religious impulse. There are also other expressions of the religious impulse, such as poetry and literature and art.

4. Niebuhr, *Christianity and Power Politics*, 6.

It is also important to note that I am using "religion" in a very broad sense that includes, in addition to the general world religions, such things as Marxism, Communism, and Humanism, because these are all attempts to articulate an ultimate frame of meaning. In my understanding, not every religion includes God, although every religion does have its god. In Communism, for example, it is the State.

So, the religious question is not one which is asked only at church or only in the context of a religious community. In this sense, the religious question is not a supernatural question; it is a natural question—in fact, it is the most natural question we can ask, one that we cannot avoid asking and answering in one way or another.

My discussion of the existential or religious question and what I have learned about its answer will be based on human reason, and I will appeal only to evidence that is generally available to any person who reflects thoroughly on human experience. I will try not to settle anything just by referring to an external authority. I will not say: "This must be true because a sacred text, or a great thinker, or the majority of people says so." This way of resolving issues never works. Someone can always legitimately ask *why* what the text or the thinker or most people say is true, why they are right. External sources solve nothing unless we give them the authority to do so. We *confer* their authority. And then the question is why we grant the power. In the end, we must all rely on our experience and our wits. There is no appeal beyond the individual bar of justification.

FAITH AND REASON

Not everyone will be comfortable with how I am proceeding. Some will argue that a purely philosophical approach to the question about life's meaning is inadequate and even inappropriate, because the answer is more a matter of believing than of thinking. Human reason and human experience are well and good in everyday matters, but when it comes to the big question about life—so the argument goes—we must rely on faith.

So, it will be helpful to talk briefly about what we mean by knowing and believing, and how they are related.

When we say we know that something is true, we mean that we actually have the evidence—or, at least we have access to the evidence—that it is true. I know that the world is not flat, because I have seen the evidence from physics, and I have even seen pictures of the world taken from space. Although I was not present when Napoleon was defeated at Waterloo, I know that it is true, because I know what counts as evidence, and I have good reasons to respect the methods and the expertise of historians.

The evidence that justifies a truth-claim is broader than just empirical or scientific evidence. Murder is wrong. The music of Bach is beautiful. I know that both statements are true, although the supporting evidence is, respectively, moral and aesthetic, not empirical. In general, then, I know something is true because I'm convinced by the appropriate evidence.

What do we mean when we say that we believe something? Here there are two possibilities: faith as an *addition* to reason, or faith as an *alternative* to reason; I believe *in* something, or I believe *that* something is true. The two senses of "believe" are expressed in Latin as *fiducia* (belief-in) or *fides* (belief-that).

Faith as *fiducia* means that I choose to act in accord with something I know to be true. I know that my wife loves me, and I choose to honor her love and be faithful to it. To take a theological example, the medieval theologian Thomas Aquinas thought that we could know the existence of God to be true, and he developed five proofs to demonstrate this. He showed that belief in God was, so to speak, reasonable. But even if someone accepts the proofs, there is no guarantee that he or she will take the additional step of trusting in God and living accordingly. For a variety of reasons—including passion, weakness, and habit—we humans don't always align our knowledge and our actions. I know that texting while driving is dangerous and illegal, but will I put the phone away?

So faith, understood as *fiducia*, trust, is entirely compatible with reason, because it is an addition to reason; it does not replace or usurp reason.

But what about *fides*? Can faith, understood as belief-that, be a legitimate alternative to reason? Should we believe that something is true, even if we cannot produce any evidence to say we know it is true? Can we believe that God exists, for example, even if we do not or cannot know that God exists?

Some thinkers say yes, *fides* is a legitimate alternative to knowledge—at least in cases where something vital (such as the existence of God or the meaning of life) is at stake, and reason cannot decide the answer.

One famous example of this faith-as-an-alternative-to-knowledge approach is the wager theory offered by the French thinker, Blaise Pascal. I do not know whether there is a God. But I can believe either that God exists or that God doesn't exist. If I believe that God does not exist, and I am right, I will never know, because I will die and that will be it. If, however, I am wrong, I will be punished forever. On the other hand, if I believe that God exists and I am right, I will be rewarded, whereas if I am wrong, I will never know. Therefore, believing that God exists is a better bet than believing that God does not exist.

A more sophisticated defense of the *fides* approach was offered by the Danish philosopher, Søren Kierkegaard, who argued that faith is a matter of passionate commitment to an objective uncertainty—faith is a leap. I can't know whether God exists, either because the evidence is absent or because it is contradictory; the matter is "objectively uncertain." In this situation, as the American philosopher William James says, we have the right to believe, because the issue is so vital, so important to our lives.

I find these defenses of the *fides* approach problematical. Pascal reduces belief in God to a utilitarian calculation of what is in my best self-interest, whereas I think belief in deity is more about falling in love and getting outside myself than placing my existential poker chips. Kierkegaard's passionate commitment is more to the point, but the "blind leap" concerns me. If faith is passionate commitment, what is to prevent me from committing myself passionately to something that is a mistake or an illusion or even something evil? Many terrorists believe passionately that indiscriminate violence is a legitimate means of furthering their cause, but their belief does not justify murder of the innocents.

Here is the key question: Is something true because we believe it, or do we believe it because it is true? Most intelligent people used to believe that the sun revolves around the earth, but they were wrong. The act of belief does not create the truth of what is believed. It should be the case, rather, that we believe something *because it is true*. But this means that there must be independent reasons—other than the fact of my belief—that make it true.

I conclude that faith (belief-that, *fides*) is not self-justifying and should not be used as an alternative to reason. Blind faith, so far as I can tell, should not be an option for us. Granted, James speaks for a lot of people when he defends their right to believe in cases where an issue is of great importance, and it cannot be resolved by reason. But I do not think that we have the right to gamble or to leap at all if a vital matter cannot be settled by careful thinking and a complete examination of our experience. Otherwise, we get in the bad habit of believing things just because we want to believe them. If reason or experience cannot settle the question of God's existence, then I think we should be agnostics.

To summarize: My position is that faith is best understood as belief-in, *fiducia*, putting our trust in something we already hold to be true through reason and experience. Faith can legitimately go beyond reason, but faith should not go around reason. We cannot settle the existential question about the meaning of life by avoiding reason and experience and appealing solely to faith.

My rationalistic bent and my strictly philosophical approach to the question of life's meaning stem from an important experience in my life. Having left the monastery where I spent my college years, I was drafted into the Army and sent to Vietnam. All that I had learned, in church and in school, about a good God directing human history came into crashing conflict with the reality of evil I was experiencing in the war. I couldn't see how to reconcile what I had been taught with what was happening on the ground. It was an intellectual, emotional, and existential crisis for me—and I decided to spend time seriously studying it at the University of Chicago after the war. Unless I was simply going to jettison them, I needed to have a step-by-step examination and justification of religious claims, an examination that appealed only to human reason and human experience. What the Bible or a theological tradition said interested me, but did not count as evidence for me. *Except by just believing it, how can I determine whether what Christians believe is true?* This was my question.

I realize that not everyone needs or can relate to the kind of linear, rational approach that I will take here. Many people prefer stories to philosophy and are more comfortable with mystery in life. We all have our own paths. But I needed this approach—desperately—and this essay reflects it. My purpose is to discuss and answer the question about life's meaning without any special pleading, using only our knowledge and our experience.

OVERVIEW

To conclude these preliminary remarks, I will preview my analysis.

Because everything we know is derived from our experience, and because what we know to be true should guide how we live, I have divided the investigation into three parts that can serve as a roadmap: Experience, Understanding, and Action.

In Chapter 2, Experience, I try to broaden our understanding of experience beyond its usual meaning of sensation. I then argue—using the expanded meaning of experience—that we all live by a basic confidence that our lives have abiding significance. In Chapter 3, Understanding, I argue that this basic confidence is not an illusion or a projection, but is an experiential response to the surrounding world. The real question, then, is not whether our lives have meaning, but what it is that makes them meaningful. I argue that neither nihilism nor atheism can really answer the question; only theism—properly understood—can do so. This is the meaning of Jesus' message that God is love. In Chapter 4, Action, I argue that we ought to live according to what is true, that is, according to the law of love.

2

Experience

SOME PEOPLE THINK THAT life is meaningless and absurd; others think that it is meaningful in the short run, but, eventually, it is meaningless; still others believe that life has an ultimate meaning. How can reasonable conversation continue when there is such fundamental disagreement? Where do we go from here?

Why not start with our experience? All our concepts—including nihilism, atheism, and theism—are derived from our interaction with the world; they are interpretations of what we experience. So, let us proceed by asking about how we experience the world, and then see whether nihilism, atheism, or theism is the best explanation of our encounter. What clues does a careful examination of our experience reveal?

BEYOND SENSATION

The problem we face, I think, is not so much a variability in how people experience reality; it is a truncated understanding of what "experience" means. For most of us, experience means primarily or even exclusively sensation: what I can see or hear or touch or smell or taste. Red, salty, cool, acrid, sharp, bright, and on and on. This is the understanding of experience that has come to dominate the Western philosophical tradition. Sensations are clear and distinct and so easily noticed. They come and go.

But there is more to experience than meets the eye. There is another layer of experience, a deeper level from which sensation itself is derived, a level which is not so easily noticed, because it is always present as dim background. Drawing attention to this second level of experience is one of the greatest contributions of the philosopher Alfred North Whitehead. Whitehead calls this second level of experience "causal efficacy;" I will refer to it simply as pre-sensory or non-sensory awareness.

Whitehead describes sensations as "handy," "definite," and "manageable," whereas pre-sensory experience is "vague," "haunting," "unmanageable," "heavy," "primitive."

The basic difference between sensory awareness and non-sensory awareness has to do with our external and internal environments. We interact with the world around us (what I am calling the external environment) through our senses: I see the lake, I feel the wind, I hear the birdsong, and so forth. The sensory information we gather provides the basis for our higher-level conscious thinking.

However, our sensory awareness of the world is not immediate; it is mediated through our bodies (what I am calling the internal environment). Sensations are a reaction to the state of our bodies. I see with my eyes. I do not see my eyes (unless I'm looking in the mirror), but when I see the world, it is with my eyes. The sensation of light and shape in the external world is a reaction to the changes in the rods and cones in my eyes. My sense of sound is an interpretation of the vibrations of the tympanic membrane in my ears. We experience the world through our bodies. I experience my body directly, and the world indirectly, through my body. The awareness of my body is a form of experience—but it is by definition not a sensory experience, because it is that from which sensation is derived. My awareness of my body is a non-sensory experience of my immediate environment.

Non-sensory awareness is affective and emotional. Our general feeling of attraction or repulsion, of well-being or malaise, our various moods, our dreams—all are a value-laden awareness of the overall states of our bodies. They are "reactions to the way externality is impressing on us its own character."[1] Our most primitive interaction with the world is affective; sensations and thoughts are derived from the initial aesthetic encounter.

We can express this expanded doctrine of experience in evolutionary terms: Human consciousness, which distinguishes us from other animals, is derived from sensory experience, which we share with other animals. Sensory experience is itself derived from our nonsensory awareness of our immediate environment—an awareness that is manifested as well by lower organisms and plants. "A jellyfish advances and withdraws, and in so doing exhibits some perception of causal relationship with the world beyond itself; a plant grows downwards to the damp earth, and upwards toward the light."[2] The non-sensory awareness shared by all living beings issues in sensations for the higher animals and, in our case, also in consciousness.

EXISTENTIAL FAITH

What does this discussion about non-sensory awareness have to do with the question of life's meaning? Just this: *When we investigate our experience to find clues about life's meaning, we should start not with consciousness or sensation, but with our non-sensory awareness from which consciousness and sensation are derived.* And here, I believe, we can make a very strong case that our fundamental reaction to the world is one of attraction and trust. We experience ourselves as parts of an encompassing whole; we are aware of a surrounding environment that contains and sustains us, and our reaction to this environment is positive. We live by an existential faith that life is worth living. Schubert Ogden calls this "primal faith," "original confidence," or "fundamental trust." They all refer to the same universal conviction that life is worth living.

Before actually making the case for existential faith, it will be helpful to see how various thinkers have described it.

1. Whitehead, *Symbolism*, 45.
2. Leclerc (quoting Whitehead), *Whitehead's Metaphysics*, 143.

- Whitehead: "At the base of our existence is the sense of 'worth'. . . . It is the sense of existence for its own sake, of existence with its own justification, of existence with its own character."[3]

- Hartshorne: "Faith on the human level is trust that the nature of things insures the appropriateness of ideals of. . .goodness, truth, and beauty, to such an extent that despite all frustrations and vexations, despite disloyalty or crassness in our fellows, despite death itself, it is really and truly better to live, and to live in accord with these ideals, than to give up the struggle in death or in cynicism."[4]

- Ogden: "Given human beings such as ourselves, faith in some mode is not an option but a necessity. We unavoidably live by faith, because we can exist at all only by somehow consenting to our own existence and to existence as such in confident trust."[5]

The evidence for existential faith is indirect and falls into three categories: intellectual, moral, and transcendental.

1. All human intellectual inquiry is an expression of trust. We act, for example, as if there is an objective world outside ourselves, as if we are not living in a dream, as if our senses deliver relatively accurate information about the external world, as if reality is knowable, ordered and insofar predictable. When we discover something that does not fit our explanatory theories, we do not give up the quest; we look for a bigger theory. "Chaos theory" is a revealing term! If we believed that the world was ultimately chaotic and unintelligible, we would not have science, nor would we try to understand anything.

None of these beliefs can be proved by reason, because reason must assume them in order to function at all. We must believe something before we can know anything. The exercise of reason is an expression of trust. As Whitehead puts it: ". . .faith in reason is

---

3. Whitehead, *Modes of Thought*, 109.

4. Hartshorne, *Reality as Social Process*, 163.

5. Ogden, "Theology and Religious Studies," *Journal of the American Academy of Religion*, 7–8.

the trust that the ultimate natures of things lie together in a harmony which excludes mere arbitrariness. It is the faith that at the base of things we shall not find mere arbitrary mystery."[6] (Earlier, I argued that blind faith [*fides*] should not replace reason; now I am also arguing that reason itself rests on faith [existential *fiducia*]. The two statements are not incompatible: Reason's investigation of its own foundation in trust should not be short-circuited by an appeal to blind belief.)

Sociologist Peter Berger speaks of our confidence that the world is ordered as a "sign of transcendence":

> "The human propensity for order is grounded in a faith or trust that, ultimately, reality is in order, all right, as it should be. Needless to say, there is no empirical method by which this faith can be tested. To assert it is itself an act of faith."

> "The most fundamental of ordering gestures, that by which a mother reassures her anxious child, is a sign of transcendence. The content of this communication will invariably be the same—Don't be afraid—everything is in order, everything is all right. The child's trust in reality is recovered, and in this trust, he will return to sleep."[7]

2. All our moral activity, every attempt to do the right thing, rests on existential faith. If we ask why it is worth our energy to struggle with moral questions, why we should spend time engaged in difficult moral deliberation, why we should be moral at all, the answer will eventually lead back to the assumed worth and dignity of life (mostly human life, but increasingly, all life). The whole point of doing the "right" thing is not to violate, but rather to respect, and, when possible, to enhance life—because life is assumed to be important and worthwhile. As Schubert Ogden puts it: "Moral thought and action are existentially possible only because their roots reach down into an underlying confidence in the abiding worth of our

6. Whitehead, *Science and the Modern World*, 23.
7. Berger, *A Rumor of Angels*, 71–72.

life."[8] Franklin Gamwell makes the same point: "Our moral hopes and strivings make no sense absent an original belief in our relation to the good, without which there could not be a moral enterprise."[9]

3. Existential faith is a transcendental. By this, I mean that we can deny it only by invoking it, only by using it against itself. If I say, for example, that life is meaningless, I intend that my statement is not meaningless. Camus himself made this point: "From the moment one says that all is nonsense, one expresses something which has sense. . . .. A literature of despair is a contradiction in terms."[10]

Transcendentals are important and instructive. "Life is meaningless," much like the statements that "everything is relative," or "there is no truth," or "we cannot know what is real" cannot be true, because it contradicts itself. "Life is meaningless" is intended to be meaningful; "everything is relative" is intended to be absolute; "there is no truth" is intended to be true; "we cannot know what is real" is intended to be a claim about reality.

Saint Augustine argued that "good" and "evil" cannot be equally fundamental concepts, because we can understand what "good" means without reference to "evil," whereas we cannot understand evil except as a corruption of good. Similarly, "meaningful" is more fundamental than "meaningless," because we can understand the former on its own terms, but the latter only in terms of the former. Negations are parasitic on affirmations.

The interior logic of transcendentals is not *merely* logical. It animates eminently practical matters. So, for example, even suicide is a tragic illustration of—not really a denial of—existential faith. Whether as a desperate attempt to lay claim on someone's attention, or as an act of ritualistic protest, or as a chosen exit from an unbearable situation, the act of suicide is an act of meaning. For one reason or another, someone decides that human dignity is better respected through death than through continued living. "Even the suicide who intentionally takes his own life implicitly affirms the ultimate

8. Ogden, *The Reality of God*, 36.
9. Gamwell, *Existence and the Good*, 125.
10. Camus, "The Riddle," 85.

meaning of his tragic choice."[11] I am reminded of a poignant scene in *The Shawshank Redemption* where an elderly ex-convict, unable to find his way in society after a lifetime in prison, carves "Brooks was here" on the ceiling beam of his rented room before he hangs himself from it.

Although this is a sad and seemingly paradoxical point, it is, I believe, profoundly true. If the most primitive level of our experience were of the worthlessness and absurdity of life, the announcement of this fact should cause no alarm and call for no particular response. "As a matter of fact, on these terms, even the hatred of life is without point and the pronouncement of life's vanity as meaningless as everything else."[12]

Intellectually, morally and logically, then, the way we live our lives reveals a deep-seated confidence. We live as if our lives matter.

Two reminders are in order. First, it is important to reiterate that fundamental trust is not itself conscious, and that our conscious beliefs can be out of sync with our underlying convictions. Thus, it is entirely possible for someone to think or say that life is meaningless, even as their actions bespeak a pre-conscious, pre-sensory conviction that life is meaningful. We can live confused lives. But, as reflective beings, we ideally seek integrity, the harmony of our conscious and unconscious beliefs.

Second, in discussing existential faith, I am making a philosophical—not a psychological—point, namely that the condition of the possibility of our living at all is trust that existence is meaningful. But the conscious recognition and appreciation of our basic trust is perhaps not possible for someone unless the psychological and developmental conditions have been laid in early childhood. Martha Nussbaum, for example, discusses the central role of love and touch for fostering trust in young children: "In order for this sense of safety to emerge, the child must be able to feel held even when not being physically held: she must come to feel that the

---

11. Ogden, *The Reality of God*, 16.
12. Ogden, *The Reality of God*, 139.

environment itself holds her."[13] One of life's tragedies is how much irreparable damage can be done so early.

Typically, the urge to lift existential faith to full consciousness is prompted by life's negative threats. Gratuitous violence. The suffering of the innocent. Rejection. Betrayal. Death. In these circumstances, we long for explicit confirmation that life is indeed worth it. As theologian Hans Küng says, "Even fundamental trust, then, is always threatened, can be revised, must be ratified, sustained, lived, acquired, endured, against all pressing doubts, in new situations, by a new decision. . .. There is no unquestionable security."[14] We live as if our lives matter, but pain and suffering and loneliness wear us down. We want reassurance that our confidence is justified. Who has not felt the force of Küng's question: "Are the identity, meaningfulness and value experienced in the act of fundamental trust really lasting? Or do chaos, absurdity, illusion, sickness, evil, and death prevail in the end? Who will have the last laugh?"[15]

One way to give conscious expression to existential faith is through philosophical investigation and rational concepts—as I am attempting to do here. But much more commonly we do it through stories, myths, the arts, religion. A creation or redemption story, a symphonic movement, powerful poetry or painting or literature—these are typical aesthetic vehicles that can re-present our existential confidence consciously so that we can appreciate it, celebrate it, and be re-assured that our lives matter. The key point here is that all these vehicles—including religion itself—are ways of voicing *something we already have*.

---

13. Nussbaum, *Upheavals of Thought*, 208.

14. Küng, *Does God Exist?*, 453.

15. Küng, *Does God Exist?*, 476.

3

Understanding

ILLUSION OR RESPONSE?

THE SHEER ACT OF living presupposes a confidence that it is worth it. But is this confidence a response to what is real or just an invention, a projection of our need for sense and security? This is a nagging question that I have thought about for years. Its persistence is due to the haunting possibility that we say our lives have meaning because we *need* them to have meaning. As Freud says in *The Future of an Illusion*, "it is a very striking fact that all this is exactly as we are bound to wish it to be."[1]

Stubborn as the question is, however, it rests on a confusion. It assumes that because we want something to be true, its purported truth is just a projection of our need. But that's like saying that because I enjoy giving my wife a gift, the only reason I give it is for my own enjoyment. That might be the case, but it doesn't have to be. Perhaps I give the gift because I love my wife, and my enjoyment of her enjoyment is a wonderful by-product.

Earlier, I reviewed the evidence—intellectual, moral, and logical—for the reality of existential faith. None of the evidence depends upon what we want or need. As Ogden puts it: "I experience the meaning of life not as something which I project on life

1. Freud, *The Future of an Illusion*, 52–53.

but as something which claims me and demands that I acknowledge it."[2] I know of no convincing, conclusive way to prove this—except to appeal to our experience. If we see and accept the evidence for existential faith, then each of us must ask: Do I experience life's meaningfulness as something that confronts and claims me, or as something that I project onto reality? Am I its creature or its creator? My position is that existential faith is true because it is inevitable, and *what is inevitable cannot be illusory.* To know something as illusory, we must also know what is real, what is outside the illusion. I know what a dream is, because I know what non-dreaming is. If existential faith is *inevitable,* then there is no way that we can step outside it to see what reality "is really like." Because existential faith is presupposed by everything we do, even by our attempts to deny it, what sense could it possibly make to say "but it might not be really true; it might just be a projection of our needs"?

This is Küng's point when he writes: "It must now be obvious that the fundamental trust in the identity, meaningfulness and value of reality, which is the presupposition of human science and autonomous ethics, is justified in the last resort only if reality itself. . .is not groundless, unsupported and aimless."[3]

The only appropriate attitude toward the necessary is acceptance and appreciation.

Existential faith is not an illusion; it is our inevitable response to reality. The question before us, therefore, is not *whether* life has meaning, but rather *what* it is that gives our life meaning. What is it about the world we experience that evinces our trust? And here, indeed, we can be confused or just plain wrong in our interpretation. Although existential faith cannot be an illusion, how we understand its grounding may indeed be an illusion.

Earlier, we saw that the existential question has three possible answers: nihilism (no meaning), atheism (limited meaning), or theism (lasting meaning). Because our existential confidence is not an illusion, but an inevitable response to what is real, we can now say that nihilism is not a valid answer. People, of course, are free to call

2. Ogden, *The Credibility of God,* 52.
3. Küng, *Does God Exist?,* 476.

themselves nihilists and to believe that life is absurd, but, according to the evidence we have been examining, their nihilism can be verbal only, and it will be contradicted by the way they actually live. Nihilism is conceptual confusion.

That leaves atheism or theism as the possible answers. Our lives have meaning, but is it temporary and proximate only, or enduring and ultimate? This, it seems to me, is *the* question: whether atheistic humanism or theism is the final truth. The answer, though it cannot be illogical, is not just a matter of logic. What counts is the explanatory power of the two proposed answers.

According to atheistic humanism, my life's meaning consists in whatever I am able to contribute to other finite beings—my children, friends, grandchildren, even humanity itself perhaps, if I am a great artist or scientist. I endure or survive in people's hearts and in their memories.

According to the theistic interpretation, the meaning of my life consists in what I contribute to other finite beings *and also* in what I contribute to a being who is everlasting. (In the Christian version, as we will see later, these amount to the same thing.) Because my contribution endures forever, it matters forever that I exist.

Which peg—atheism or theism—better bears the weight of existential faith?

This answer will not be decided by some simple, decisive proof. Otherwise, either atheists or theists would be not only wrong, but also fools. No, the case for atheism or for theism is difficult, because we are struggling to provide the best interpretation of the deepest regions of our experience. We should test the strongest form of each proposed answer according to its internal consistency and its explanatory power: How well does it illumine the depths of our experience? Are there areas of experience left unexplained?

Thus, for example, Ogden writes that "the question between the Marxist and the Christian which seems to me to be *the* question is not whether God exists in quite the way in which that question is often raised, but rather, which of these alternative ways of accounting for our fundamental confidence in the worth of life, in fact, does most justice to our experience of ourselves and our world, leaves fewer questions unanswered, brings more of our experience into some kind of an integrity and unity, and so on."[4]

Arguments for and against theism are also complicated—as I will show—by our presuppositions about what "God" means. I am trying to work backward from our experience of the world to an interpretation of reality that explains that experience, but people may resist a turn toward the theistic interpretation, because they have a preconceived idea of what "God" refers to, and they don't want to go there.

My position is that the theistic alternative is the better answer to the question of life's meaning, *provided the reality of God is coherently conceived*. To say that "there is a God" is to say that our confidence in the final meaning of our lives is justified by the character of reality. The universe is neither hostile nor indifferent toward us; it is benevolent.

All of this, of course, must be argued, and not just asserted.

THE OBJECTIVE GROUND OF
EXISTENTIAL FAITH

A good way to make the argument is to begin by asking what an adequate grounding of existential faith would look like. We live by a trust that our lives make a difference; the ill and the good that we do matters. Even if nobody sees my actions, they count and even if everyone forgets my actions, they count. When my distant descendants no longer remember who I was, it still matters that I lived and how I lived. This is the driving energy of existential faith.

To say that existential faith is a response to reality, therefore, is to say that the ground of our confidence must be both supremely sensitive and supremely stable. Reality must be exquisitely attuned to every nuance of my hopes and fears, my struggles and decisions, and at the same time be rock-solid in its reliability. The ground of our confidence must be both the infinite register of our lives and also "the great anchor that cannot drag."[5] The encompassing whole

4. Ogden, *The Credibility of God*, 53.

5. Hartshorne, *Reality as Social Process*, 207.

must be both changing in response to our actions and changeless in its constancy.

In both regards—sensitivity and stability—atheistic humanism falls short as an adequate explanatory ground of existential faith. If the beings who understand and value my life are themselves all finite, then there will be aspects of my life that are missed, aspects that are not fully understood, and aspects that are forgotten. The register of my life will necessarily be inadequate and incomplete. And finally, the anchor will drag. My life will be entirely forgotten when there is no longer anyone to remember it. It will be as if I never existed. The same may be said of the entire human species. For atheistic humanism, there will come a time when the horrors of the Holocaust no longer matter. The human story will not only be ended; it will be erased in an impersonal universe.

Necessarily absent in the atheistic interpretation is the sense that my life has enduring significance, because it contributes to something that abides forevermore. While atheistic humanism is correct to emphasize the importance of human life and the necessity of action now, in this world, to undo injustice and to expand human possibilities, in the end its worldview cannot fully support the intuitive power of existential faith. Despite frustration, despite our death, despite the eventual evaporation of our entire species, *it matters that we are here.*

I conclude that theism—rather than nihilism or atheism—provides the only worldview capable of fully grounding existential faith. This is, in effect, an argument for the existence of God based not on sacred texts or blind faith or an illusion, but on our inevitable non-sensory experience of the world. Speaking of "the proper use or function of the word 'God,'" Schubert Ogden writes:

> "I hold that the use of this word is to refer to the objective ground in reality itself of what I have called basic confidence in the worth of life. It lies in the nature of this basic confidence to affirm that the real whole of which we experience ourselves and others to be parts is such as to be worthy of, and thus itself to evoke in us, this very confidence. The word 'God,' then, serves to designate whatever it is about this experienced whole that calls

forth and justifies our original and inalienable trust in life's worth. Thus, the meaning of the word 'God' is existential and may be expressed in the words once proposed by William James: 'You can dismiss certain kinds of fear,' namely, the kinds of fear which overtake you when you are led to ask why your life is, after all, worth living. It follows that to be free of such fear by existing in this trust is one and the same with affirming the reality of God."[6]

We need to proceed carefully here. To say that there is a God is, so far, just to say that nihilism and atheism are inadequate world views. But it prompts the question of what "God" properly means. And there is certainly no lack of idolatrous candidates—false gods such as wealth, fame, power, gender, race, country, or species that lay claim to, although they are entirely unworthy of, our ultimate loyalty. The horrors of history all have the same logic: God is on my side.

Even traditionally orthodox understandings of "God" can be seriously problematic. As I write, there has been a natural gas explosion at a Christian academy in a nearby major city. Two employees have been killed, but because it is summer, no classes were in session. In a news report, someone refers to the fortunate lack of student deaths as "God's protection plan." The concept of God underlying this statement is, I will argue, extremely problematic—nonsensical, even—and this accounts for the persistence of much atheism in our culture. Even though it cannot provide an adequate explanation for our basic faith, atheism endures because a lot of theism just doesn't make sense, and actually ought to be rejected.

THE PROBLEM OF EVIL

Where was God at Auschwitz? I will use the problem of evil as an entry point to criticize the traditional Christian idea of God in Western thought, and to offer an alternative understanding of deity that I have found to be coherent and compelling. It was, as I indicated

---

6. Ogden, *The Reality of God*, 37.

earlier, the question of evil that drove me into the graduate study of theology in the first place.

The clearest formulation of the problem of evil was given by the eighteenth-century Scottish philosopher, David Hume. It is, says Hume, a compatibility problem, a disconnect among several things that we say are true. The Christian God is understood to be all-good, all-knowing, and all-powerful, and yet there is evil in our world. How can this be? If God were all-good and all-knowing, but not all-powerful, we could explain why there is evil. Or if God were all-good and all-powerful, but not all-knowing, we could understand. Or all-knowing and all-powerful, but not all-good. But how can we say that God is omniscient, omnipotent, and perfectly good—and yet horrific evil occurs?

It helps as a first step to distinguish moral evil from natural or physical evil, and to discuss them separately. Moral evil is the evil that results from human agency, such as violence and hatred, whereas natural evil includes such non-intentional events as disease, weather disasters, and accidents. Theodicy is the attempt to reconcile the reality of God with the reality of moral evil and natural evil.

Let's start with natural evil.

The first thing to say is that some natural evil (for example, a massive oil spill that kills wildlife) is really the result of human agency. Some cancers are the result of human activity. Some car accidents are the result of drunk driving. So, sometimes what we call natural evil is really a consequence of moral evil.

Another accounting of natural evil has to do with what it means to exist at all. To exist is to express some form of freedom. God is the ultimate form of creativity, and all non-divine beings are lesser forms of creativity (self-determination within limits). Human beings express a very high form of creativity. Subatomic particles are a minimal—but real—expression of creativity (Heisenberg's uncertainty principle is an illustration of this point).

In a universe populated with free agents, conflict is inevitable. What is good for the cancer is bad for the human. Genuine accidents will occur. The only way to avoid all conflict is to imagine a deterministic universe, totally without freedom, but that alternative is truly meaningless.

Finally, we must remember that all non-divine beings are temporally finite; only God is everlasting. Our lives have beginnings and ends. The fact that we die is not evil; it is an expression of our finitude. Time fades and alternatives exclude. Tragedy is an inevitable part of existence, and, in this sense, natural evil is compatible with the existence of God.

The more difficult question concerns moral evil.

Most of us are probably familiar with two theodicies that we learned as children. The first is that evil is God's punishment for sin, and the second is that evil serves some purpose in the divine plan. For example, it is God's way of testing us or of developing our character. Both theodicies are primitive, and both fail. If evil is punishment for sin, the penalty is not well-correlated with the crime. The young Jewish believer, Anne Frank, dies in a death camp, while the Nazi Angel of Death, Joseph Mengele, dies in his sleep, an old man in Brazil. To claim that evil serves some higher divine purpose is just to say that the end justifies the means, which is ethically wrong whether we say it about humans or about God. And, anyway, if we think that evil is part of God's plan, then we should stop trying to eliminate it.

A more substantial and promising theodicy is the free will defense first proposed by St. Augustine. A world populated by free beings is better than a world without freedom. The exercise of freedom allows also for the abuse of freedom. Tragically, human beings often abuse their freedom. The result is moral evil—for which we, not God, are responsible.

This all seems to make sense, until we try to square it with how we understand God's knowledge and power. Traditionally, divine omniscience has been interpreted as God's comprehensive knowledge of everything that has happened and everything that will happen. God knows everything that I have done and everything that I will do before I do it. Strictly speaking, temporal terms such as "has" and "will" do not really apply to God who is understood to exist outside of time, in eternity. God knows everything simultaneously, eternally. As a rough analogy, imagine a pilot who is able to see an entire mountain range all at once from above, while a hiker below will see only one peak after another as they are progressively revealed. In philosophical terms, God knows *all* past, present and future *as actual*, whereas we know (only *a tiny bit* of) the past as actual, and (only *a tiny bit* of) the future *as possible*.

Traditionally, divine omnipotence has been interpreted to mean that God has maximal power and can do anything that is not impossible (even God cannot square a circle). God is in control of history and destiny, so that whatever happens is according to God's will and is part of the divine plan.

But now we do have a serious problem. If, for example, God knows from eternity about the actuality of the terrorist attacks on September 11th, 2001, then their not happening has always been impossible since divine knowledge is infallible. Further, if God had the power to prevent the attacks, but did not, what should we conclude, except that the terrorist attacks were the will of God? Osama bin Laden carried out the divine plan.

The Augustinian free will defense really does not provide a coherent theodicy that reconciles the existence of moral evil with the reality of God. Indeed, it is hard to understand what free will even means if God knows our decisions before we make them. A considerable amount of theological ink has been spilled over the centuries trying to jerry-rig the meanings of divine omniscience and human freedom so that they fit together. So, for example, it is argued that we can throw a ball in the air and know before it happens that it will hit the ground. Thus God can know our actions before we do them. But, the ball's falling to the ground is knowable in advance precisely because it is not a free action; it is determined by the laws of physics. What is bound to happen can indeed be known before it happens. The sun will rise tomorrow—guaranteed. The question is how anyone can know in advance and for sure an action that is said to occur *freely*.

Well, it will be argued, it says in the New Testament that Jesus knew beforehand that Judas would betray him, and yet Judas did so freely. Likewise, I can know in advance that my friend will vote Democratic, but my knowledge does not negate my friend's free choice. So it is with God's foreknowledge and human free will.

What these examples show is that some actions of free agents are relatively predictable, because the agents have developed character traits that guide the way they do things. Most of us act in ways that are generally predictable (or our regular unpredictability is itself predictable), and so someone who knows us well can gauge fairly accurately how we will perform in certain situations. But even habitual actions are not *absolutely* predictable, because we can always act out of character. A lifelong smoker, whose freedom has diminished to nearly zero, can yet choose to quit. Even if a particular decision is certain to occur, there will still be some freedom about just how it will be carried out. The point is that so long as there is even an ounce of freedom associated with a choice, the decision in all its details is not absolutely necessary, and so cannot be known in advance with absolute certainty.

Another tactic is to shift the meaning of free will from "having the power to do otherwise" to "doing what you want to do." If God knows from eternity what our choices are even before we make them, this line of reasoning goes, then we don't have the power to do anything other than what God already knows to be true, but we still make our choices freely because we are doing what we want to do. We are predestined but also preprogrammed to want our only available "choice." But I think this is nonsense, and not really freedom at all. Imagine that I drug you and lock you in a room from which you cannot escape. You awake, enjoy where you are, and decide to stay. Are you free? Yes, if you mean by freedom "doing what I want to do," but no, if freedom means "having the power to do otherwise." My answer is that you are not really free; you are just lucky because you want to do the only thing that it is possible for you to do.

The final fallback position for some people at this point is to invoke mystery: We can't fully understand how an all-good, all-knowing, and all-powerful being can allow evil, or how our freedom of choice is compatible with divine foreknowledge, but this is because our minds are limited and so incapable of comprehending infinite mystery. The alternative conclusion, of course, is the one that Hartshorne wryly draws: A mystery is what a contradiction becomes when we say it about God, rather than something else.

In any case, if it is all a mystery anyway, then silence is the only appropriate theology. We shouldn't say anything at all about God's will or a divine plan.

Theodicy's failure to resolve the problem of moral evil illustrates an important point: Even though theism, rather than nihilism or atheism, seems the most reasonable option for grounding existential faith, it, too, is beset with serious difficulties. Theism, it seems, is no less confused and contradictory than atheism or nihilism.

The real problem with the free-will defense is the muddled idea of God that it presupposes.

Specifically, the traditional interpretations of omniscience and omnipotence are based on bad thinking. Omniscience means perfect knowledge of everything, exactly as it is. A perfect knower would know all the actualities of the past completely. Perfect memory would differ from our memory in two senses: Whereas we know only a very small portion of the entire past (mostly connected with our own histories, much of which we still forget), God would know absolutely every detail of the history of the entire universe. And a perfect knower would remember each actual past event in its full richness. We finite beings remember very few events completely, and those we do so remember are remarkable. I can remember exactly where I was, what I was doing, how I felt when I heard of the assassination of John Kennedy, when I saw the Challenger explosion, when I heard about the September 11th attacks. Imagine a being who could remember every detail of the entire past even more vividly. It would be as if the past continued to live in the divine memory.

How would a perfect knower know the future? The formal answer is: God would know the future exactly as it is. So, how is the future—is it actual or is it possible? We certainly face the future as if it were the realm of possibilities among which we will choose, rather than the realm of actualities that are already determined, like the past flipped forward. Our whole notion of personal responsibility depends upon our conviction that the future is more like clay for us to mold than like the second half of the movie that we have not yet watched. We experience the past as actual, but the future as possible.

If, however, God knows the future as actual (as the traditional notion of omniscience requires), and if God is the perfect knower, then the future *is* actual, and our experience of it as possible is an anthropomorphic illusion. Everything is predestined, and there is no personal responsibility. But rather than accept this counterintuitive conclusion that would require scrapping our legal system and building shrines to dictators who are carrying out God's will, why not just admit that we are not thinking clearly?

If the future is the realm of possibilities, then a perfect knower would know the future *as possible.* The difference between our knowledge and God's is that God knows all the possibilities (we know very few) and all in their relative weights—what is more or less likely. But even a perfect knower does not know with absolute certainty what a free being will choose, until the choice is made and becomes part of the immediate past.

Omniscience, properly conceived, means perfect knowledge of the past as actual and of the future as possible.

What about omnipotence? The monopolistic model is entirely inappropriate. If human beings have *some* decision-making power, then God does not have *all* of it. "All-powerful" or "perfect power" refer to quality as well as quantity: God has the highest quality of power that is consistent with there being other agents who have some power. Here a social model of power is more helpful. Power is understood in terms of persuasion rather than coercion. Yes, I can put a gun to your head and demand that you open the safe, but there is no way I can force you to respect me or love me. Not even omnipotence can completely override free will.

In a social model of power, one agent influences another noncoercively, through inspiration and judgment. A leader can motivate people to follow freely. A respected friend's disappointment with my decision may cause me to change future actions. Omnipotence means supreme social influence over other agents—influence that respects and does not override their freedom.

Here, then, is a theodicy that works: Human beings have free will, even though it is often severely limited by their past actions and by their neighbors. God knows perfectly everything that we have done and everything that we may or may not do. God's influence over us is through persuasion and judgment, not via coercive intrusions into the human drama. Moral evil exists because we ignore or reject divine urging and divine reaction and choose instead to act in ways that are destructive. God cannot prevent moral evil because God does not have all the decision-making power. As a French theologian expressed it: Thou hast created me creator of myself.

It follows that not everything that happens is the will of God, because God does not determine the details of history. As Hartshorne puts it: "Perhaps there is no 'why' God sends us evils, since he does not send them at all. Rather, he establishes an order in which creatures can send each other particular goods and evils."[7]

CLASSICAL AND NEOCLASSICAL THEISM

These reinterpretations of omniscience and omnipotence are part of an overall rethinking of the idea of deity that has been carefully and convincingly worked out by the philosophers Alfred North Whitehead and Charles Hartshorne. Called neoclassical (or process) theism, this idea of God is presented as an alternative to classical theism, the traditional way of thinking about God.

From the beginning, Christian theology has been an exercise in faith seeking understanding of itself through dialogue with culture. Theologians have engaged the best thinking of their time to grasp and to explain the meaning of their faith. What I am calling classical theism is the mainline Western understanding of God that employed the insights of classical Greek philosophy—chiefly, Aristotle—to explain the biblical idea of God. The main spokesperson of classical theism was the thirteenth-century Dominican monk Thomas Aquinas, whose impressive *Summa Theologica* was a comprehensive exposition of Christian theology in Aristotelian philosophical categories.

At the risk of oversimplification, I will say that the main insight driving Greek thought and the classical idea of God is the preference for being over becoming. Being is primary, becoming secondary. Why does classical thought privilege being over

7. Hartshorne, *A Natural Theology for Our Time*, 120.

becoming? Becoming—the world we inhabit—is the realm of time, change, decay, and death. We come into existence and we pass away. The realm of being, on the other hand, is eternal, changeless, incorruptible, perfect. Our existential security, therefore, depends on our somehow exiting the world of becoming and entering (or re-entering) the world of being. The Greek doctrine of the immortality of the soul and the Christian teaching about the resurrection of the body are two interpretations of how humans transcend the world of becoming and attain the world of being.

God, on the classical model, exists outside of time in eternity and is entirely changeless. God is pure being. Our discussion of theodicy and the problem of evil illustrates some of the problems with this view of God. The central difficulty is how a being who is conceived to be eternal and absolute can in any meaningful sense be said to be related to us, since relations involves change. God, classically conceived, simply cannot ground existential faith.

As Fr. David Tracy put the point in *Blessed Rage for Order*:

> "All reflective persons should, then, investigate the process thinkers' charge that the major affirmation of the classical Christian theological tradition, namely its understanding of God, may be missing the point of the scriptural understanding of God's relationship to man. . .. My own suspicion is that all authentic Christians live and pray and speak as if God were really affected by their action. They live as if, to use the expression of one process theologian, God really were Pure Unbounded Love struggling, suffering, achieving with humanity. Yet the question recurs: Christians may live and say this, but can they *mean* it? Can they render it conceptually coherent if they continue to employ the concepts of classical theology? Can Christians mean the most fundamental religious affirmation of Christian self-understanding if they simultaneously affirm the usual understanding of classical Christianity that God is the self-subsistent, changeless, omniscient, all-powerful one who is not really. . . affected by human actions?"[8]

8. Tracy, *Blessed Rage for Order*, 177.

We admire a mother whose love for her children is adjusted to their differing needs and who shares intimately in their sorrows and joys. Such a mother is not changeless—nor would we want her to be. An unaffected, changeless parent is a poor parent. If, ordinarily, love means being really related to and affected by the beloved, then supreme love would not mean being *un*related and *un*affected, but, rather, being *supremely* related and *supremely* affected. Neoclassical theism offers an alternative view of the divine reality: Love involves change, and so a loving God changes.

Classical theism understands God as entirely changeless, but it is a mistake to think that neoclassical theism just substitutes an idea of God as entirely changing. Rather, the neoclassical understanding is *dipolar*: God is changing in some respects and changeless in other respects.

A couple of examples illustrate what "dipolar" means. Is a mother's wonderful love for her children changing or changeless? The answer is: both. In its *concrete expression*, her love is changing; it is adapted to the specific and differing needs of each of her children. But in its *abstract quality* or its intensity, her love is changeless. Her love for Jane is different from her love for John, because Jane and John are different, but she loves them both the same.

Another example: Am I the same person I was fifty years ago? Yes and no. I am the same person, but I have changed. How can both be true without contradiction? Well, what is different about me are the different states in which I exist—Larry happy, Larry sad, Larry teaching, Larry reading, Larry sleeping, Larry young, Larry old, Larry working, Larry retired. But throughout all these different concrete states run the constant abstract features that identify Larry as Larry—male, interested in ideas, enjoying nature, and so forth. My identity is an abstraction from my various concrete manifestations; my identity is expressed in and through my diverse concrete states.

The central neoclassical insight is that being and becoming are not invidious; one is not better or "deeper" or "more real" than the other. Becoming and its synonyms such as change and relatedness are not inferior ways of existing. Being and becoming are, rather, complementary features of reality, so that neither makes sense in isolation from the other. The world of becoming is, as the Greeks said, the world of time and change. But the realm of being is not something *outside* of time and change, but *within it.* (This is why Whitehead and Hartshorne prefer "everlasting" to "eternal.") Being is contained within becoming, and changelessness is contained within change, as the abstract is contained in the concrete.

God's perfection is not "all being and no becoming," but rather the highest form of being *and* the highest form of becoming. God is both supremely changeless and supremely changing, necessary and contingent, absolute and related, abstract and concrete. The logic of all these conceptual pairs is exactly the same: Both are required to understand either, and one is included within the other. So, for example, what is necessary is what all contingent possibilities have in common, what will unfailingly happen in any contingent circumstance. God's perfection is the supreme form of each polar opposite: For example, God is supremely related to all others, and insofar supremely absolute, because God's relatedness to all others is itself not relative to anything.

This dipolar conception of deity provides a grounding of existential faith that maintains and explains its twin intuitions of sensitivity and stability. Deity is perfectly related to all non-divine reality and this relatedness is itself perfectly absolute. My life—and all of reality—are perfectly included and preserved in a being that endures forever.

GOD AND THE WORLD

One helpful way of picturing this new understanding of God is Hartshorne's image of *the world as God's body*, a phrase that recalls Plato's notion of the world as "the living garment of deity" and St. Paul's reference to the God "in whom we live, and move, and have our being."

In *Man's Vision of God*, Hartshorne carefully works out the meaning of this powerful image by combining two analogies, the organic (mind-body) analogy and the social (person-to-person) analogy. I know/feel my body immediately, and I act on or control my (properly functioning) body directly. To move my hand, I simply will to do so, and it happens.

How do we know and influence other human beings? I can never know another person, even through sexual intimacy, immediately, the way I know my own body. All knowledge of other persons is indirect and mediated; it is our experience of their experience. I feel your feelings through imagination and sympathetic response. Similarly, we cannot control other persons the way we can control our own bodies. Our ability to affect or truly move other free agents is not through manipulation or coercion, but rather through persuasion and inspiration. (A totalitarian regime may keep people in line by treating them as objects, but it cannot force their loyalty or respect.)

The organic analogy gives us immediacy and intimacy; the social analogy gives us relationality and respect. Imagine, then, a social relation that is intimately immediate. *God knows the world as intimately as we know our own bodies, and acts on the world as directly as we act on our own bodies—but through inspiration rather than manipulation.* The world is God's body, and God is the abstract identity (soul, mind) in world process.

We should pause to consider the implications of this powerful image. The first thing it shows is that our relation to deity, although social, is not the same as our relation to another human person, even an incomparably large and important other person. Our relation to other persons is like the relation between cells in our body, but our relation to God is analogous to a cell's relation to its host body. We experience deity, not as a distinct other, but as the *environment* "within which we live and move and have our being." We are, so to speak, the "cells" in God's body.

This means that our awareness of God is constant but vague and indistinct. We catch a glimpse of deity only out of the corner of our eye. We experience deity as the *background* of everything else we experience, analogous to the way we experience our bodies in our sensory experience of the external world. We experience God as the *horizon* within which we experience everything else. Our primal awareness of deity is not something sensory or mystical; it is the underlying conviction that our lives matter, that we have worth, that we are safe in the encompassing whole, that we are loved. Existential faith is the experience of God.

HOW GOD ACTS IN THE WORLD

"The world as God's body" also helps us understand how God acts in the world. If we, the parts of the body, have some measure of freedom and creativity, then God's making our local decisions is both inappropriate and nonsensical—as if God both shares power and yet has all of it, as if we were to intervene directly in the cellular activity of our bodies. The proper divine role, rather, is to set the environmental rules within which any local decisions can be made at all. By "environmental rules" I mean the optimal limits within which free decisions can be made, and by "optimal limits" I mean the boundaries that maximize the chances of success over failure.

The parent-child analogy is helpful here. Parents want to teach children how to make good decisions. Initially, this means that parents make the decisions for the child, but as the child develops, good parents will set boundaries within which the child begins to make her own decisions—boundaries that are wide enough to allow for real decisions, but not so broad as to invite danger and chaos. Little Mary is free to play anywhere in her own back yard, but she is not allowed to wander down the street by herself. As the child matures, the limits are appropriately widened.

One way God acts in the world, then, is by setting the limits, the rules, within which the human adventure occurs. The laws of nature are an example.

A second way that God acts in the world is by saving us from insignificance. Rather than simply perishing with our passing, our hopes and dreams, our struggles and decisions, our successes and failures are all "rescued" by God. They are felt perfectly and preserved perfectly in the divine reality where they live forevermore. This "objective immortality" in the divine memory is what guarantees—for good or ill—the everlasting significance of our actions.

There is a third way to understand divine action in history. In feeling our feelings, God is also free to react. As the soul or mind in world process, God's evaluative reaction to the decisions of the parts is based on what is best for the whole. God feels our feelings, and we in turn feel God's evaluative reaction to our decisions. In this way, God can influence us through inspiration, persuasion, and judgment. I cannot improve upon Hartshorne's explanation:

> "Then to alter us he has only to alter himself. God's unique power over us is his partly self-determined being as our inclusive object of awareness. . . .God, as self-determined, is the essential object of our awareness. . . .We enjoy God's enjoyment of ourselves. This enjoyment-of-being-enjoyed is the essential factor in all our enjoyment. . . . we influence God by our experiences but do not thereby deprive him of freedom in his response to us. This divine response, becoming our object, by the same principle in turn influences us, but here, too, without removing all freedom. . . .Thus God can rule the world and order it, setting optimal limits for our free action, by presenting himself as essential object, so characterized as to weight the possibilities of response in the desired respect. This divine method of world control is called 'persuasion' by Whitehead and is one of the greatest of all metaphysical discoveries, largely to be credited to Whitehead himself. He, perhaps the first of all, came to the clear realization that it is by molding himself that God molds us, by presenting at each moment a partly new ideal or order of preference which our unself-conscious awareness takes as object, and thus renders influential upon our entire activity."[9]

Our experience of deity thus includes our awareness of God's reaction to our choices and God's urging us toward the good. This is the core meaning of conscience—that persistent voice within that holds us to account and beckons our better angels.

This interpretation of divine action in the world also helps us understand the meaning of prayer. One thing prayer certainly does not mean is begging (or reminding) God to do something that God would not do otherwise. "Please, God, protect my son in the combat zone!" As heartfelt, understandable, and therapeutic as such a

9. Hartshorne, *The Divine Relativity*, 139–42.

plea is, do we imagine that, without the prayer, the God who loves us unconditionally would ignore my son? Such a prayer may also be inappropriate if it supposes that God intervenes—through our special pleading—to override natural laws or human decisions. Martin Luther observed that "we pray, not to instruct God, but to instruct ourselves," and this better articulates the meaning of prayer. We pray, in the first instance, to recall the presence of God, to raise to consciousness our unconscious awareness of our theistic environment. We pray in thanksgiving that our lives have been redeemed from meaninglessness and insignificance. We pray to commit ourselves to working on behalf of the good. We pray to increase our sensitivity, to search our conscience, to ascertain what God wishes for the world and for us now. We pray to discern the divine reaction to our decisions. Using the Catholic image of the "mystical body of Christ," we pray that other parts of the body— persons, groups, nations—become increasingly conscious of what it means to do the right thing and have the courage to do so. All of which means, of course, that we pledge to do our important part to help make this happen. The fate of human history is a joint enterprise. God does God's part, and we must do ours.

SUMMARY

Existential faith is universal and inevitable in human life and, therefore, it is objectively grounded in external reality, because it is a response to our environment, to the whole of which we perceive ourselves to be parts. What is the character of reality, how shall we understand it, if trust is our inevitable response? Nihilism gives an inconsistent answer, atheism is inadequate, and classical theism is incoherent.

Neoclassical theism provides a reasonable alternative, a way to ground existential faith that makes sense. With its dipolar conception of deity and its analogy of the world as God's body, it provides a coherent theodicy and an intelligible rendering of what it means to say that God acts in history, as well as what we mean by conscience and prayer. Sadly, this new theistic understanding remains largely ignored in the popular press. Atheists such as E.O. Wilson and Richard Dawkins show no awareness of it and continue to rail against classical theism as if it were the only possible concept of God. This is unfortunate, because neoclassical thought addresses atheistic concerns and presents a persuasive theistic interpretation of our common human experience. It would be instructive to see the atheistic response to *this* form of theism.

JESUS

The philosophical portrait of God that I have been sketching was extremely important to me as a student trying to work through the problem of evil and find something to hold on to. To this day, I continue to find the writings of Whitehead, Hartshorne, and Ogden deeply moving. Their intellectual rigor, clarity, and honesty inspire and motivate me. They help me make sense of my experience. They challenge me to try to live in a certain way.

I realize, however, that most people are not especially moved by philosophical argument; most of us relate more to stories and examples than to reflections. In this regard, the gospel account of Jesus and his proclamation of the God of love is much more powerful than philosophical analyses. Christians believe that in the story of Jesus of Nazareth the full face of God which we always already have known—but through a glass darkly—is fully disclosed as pure unbounded love.

Before talking further about Jesus, we need to stand back for a moment and take stock of where we are in this discussion. Our investigation of human experience has led us to the reality of a being who is conceived to be supremely sensitive to all others and supremely active for the good of all others—as good a philosophical understanding of "perfect love" as one could imagine. In this sense, reason is capable of arriving at the existence of a loving God.

Furthermore, reason is capable of determining the appropriate response, the right way to live if we come from, are supported by, and return to the love of God. We should celebrate and dwell completely in this truth, and so be liberated from all our fears and failures through the realization that we are always held in love, that our lives have final significance no matter what happens. That we are safe. Completely safe. The "reasonable" response to unconditional love is to give ourselves over to it completely, to trust in it alone, and to be loyal to it in all our dealings with others.

So, it seems that "philosophy all by itself already sees what the New Testament says." Philosophy can arrive at the existence of God and can counsel us to live our lives according to that truth. But if all this is accessible to reason, why is revelation necessary? Why do we need Jesus?

On one level, it is because, even though it is *capable* of arriving at the truth, reason doesn't necessarily do so. I pointed out above that we humans have a problem understanding who we really are. Our conscious thoughts do not always mirror our existential faith. Nihilism and atheism, for example, are confused forms of self-understanding. In a world in which we are offered so many misleading and inadequate interpretations of what it means to be fully human (check out the self-help section of any bookstore), it is important to have the right interpretation made explicitly clear to us.

As unfortunate and distracting as conceptual confusion is, however, it is not the end of the world. People can still live good lives even if their ideas are jumbled. The deeper problem is not so much that we are confused in our self-understanding; it is that we are inauthentic in how we choose to live.

Here is the curious reality: Although putting our trust in God alone makes "complete sense," we *don't* trust God completely; we don't give ourselves over to the divine reality entirely. We put our trust and our loyalty in something other than, or at least alongside, God. We invest something finite—self, power, wealth, nation, race—with final meaning. In one way or another, we fall for an idol; we choose to live inauthentically.

That we make this profound mistake over and over is absolutely clear to me from human history—and from my own story. *Why* we do it is a great mystery. Maybe it is just too hard to reorder our priorities and live in loyalty to divine love. Perhaps it's because we panic as we wrestle with our finitude and face our death. Life is a bumpy ride and we want to take the wheel. Perhaps we just don't like being a small side show rather than the main event: it's all too much about God and not enough about me. Or, perhaps, it's because we seek to evade the terrible responsibility that authenticity demands, and so we try to lose ourselves in others.

The real human problem—called "sin" in the Christian tradition—is our resistance to what is true, our continuing to live falsely even when the truth is plainly disclosed to us. I live with the underlying conviction that my life is meaningful. In their different ways, careful philosophical reflection and the proclamation of Jesus both disclose life's meaning to be rooted in the divine reality. But I insist on seeking my meaning, my grounding, elsewhere: in self, fame, fortune, nation, etc. We misunderstand ourselves not only through intellectual confusion, but also—and more radically—through willful denial of that which we know on the most fundamental level to be true. The truth is that the part exists for the sake of the whole, but we want to live as if the whole exists for the sake of the part.

A central theme in the Christian tradition is thus that we need to *be* saved, to *be* redeemed. We cannot do it on our own. The possibility of authentic self-understanding is available to us in every moment—because we are held in God's love every moment—but we seem unable to realize it on our own. Authentic life becomes possible only when we are somehow delivered from ourselves. Although philosophy can understand the human condition, it cannot solve the human predicament. Even though philosophy at its best can show us what is true, its summons to live accordingly is not effective. What we require is not just correct understanding, but a change of heart. For that we need a historical prompt, an existential confrontation, a human life that shows us the way and forces us to decide whether we will follow.

For Christians, it is Jesus of Nazareth who proclaims the truth and challenges us to decide if we will live accordingly. He is the decisive revelation of God in history. The Kingdom of God is at hand! Change your ways! This means, as Ogden puts it, that "what confronts us in Jesus is not. . .a 'world-view' addressed to our intellects, but a possibility of self-understanding that requires of us a personal decision."[10] The revelation of Jesus is not a body of timeless philosophical truths, but an existential challenge that demands decision. The difference between philosophy and proclamation is the difference between abstract knowledge *about* something and concrete experience *of* something. So, for example, there is a big difference between understanding what "friendship" means and actually having a friend, or between understanding what "forgiveness" means and actually being forgiven. Jesus' proclamation is directed at our hearts, not our heads. In this sense, Jesus is humanity's preacher, as well as its teacher.

Before unpacking what "decisive revelation" means, an important caveat is in order. Jesus is the decisive revelation of God *for Christians*, but not necessarily the *exclusive* revelation of God. Jews, Muslims, Hindus, Buddhists and others claim different prophets and teachers as decisive for their worldviews. We are historical beings, and so we are not religious in general any more than we speak language in general. When we speak it is through one or another specific language, and when we existentially encounter ultimate reality it is through one or another particular religious tradition and its prophet(s). To be a Christian is to say that in the story of Jesus I have met God. For Christians, Jesus is the full revelation of God as love, with all that this implies about our acceptance by God, our gratitude to God, and our obligation to others.

Does this mean that all religions, or at least the great world religions, are on an equal footing? I don't know. I haven't studied—inhabited, really—other traditions sufficiently to have an informed opinion. But I do know that insofar as any tradition has a legitimate path to ultimate reality, all its members are anonymous Christians, just as all Christians would be anonymous members of that tradition. It is at least possible that although the *revealer* is different in different traditions, the *revealed* is the same. If the God revealed by Jesus is the true God, then any other true revelation of God will bear the same substantive marks as Jesus' revelation. For me this means that any true revelation will be about love as the final truth. Ultimacy trumps perspectivism.

---

10. Ogden, *Christ Without Myth*, 162.

REVELATION AS RE-PRESENTATION

What, then, does it mean to say that Jesus is the revelation of God? We can understand revelation in two different ways. On one interpretation, it means the disclosure of unknown, esoteric, or secret knowledge. The revealer shows us something that we would not have known otherwise. In this sense I might reveal to you my computer password.

The other interpretation is that revelation means a re-presentation of something we already know, but only partially or dimly or confusedly. Rather than showing us a new truth, revelation in this second sense means clarification or crystallization, making explicit what was previously implicit, focusing in the foreground what had been hidden in the background. I look at a field of data over and over, and suddenly an explanatory pattern pops out. I've looked so many times before, but only now do I see.

It is in this second sense that Jesus is said to be the revelation of God. The Christian tradition has been clear and consistent on this point, as illustrated by its early rejection of Gnosticism (which taught that Jesus' revelation consisted of new esoteric knowledge) and its embrace of Paul's message (Romans 1:19) that "all that may be known about God lies plain before their eyes."

To re-present something is literally to present it again, a second time. Christian theology thus distinguishes between God's *original* or *general* self-disclosure in nature and conscience and God's *special* revelation through Jesus. Jesus makes obvious what has been there all along. In this sense, what Jesus reveals is not something new, but something everlastingly true that has been made consciously new *for me*. In terms that I am using in this essay, Jesus re-presents clearly what we are always experiencing dimly through existential faith. It is in this sense that Jesus reveals God. "Yet we should remember that it is revelation only as climbing an eminence affords us a prospect because the landscape is there already."[11] Ogden puts the point this way: "The possibility of self-understanding that Jesus decisively re-presents is the authentic possibility implicitly

---

11. Oman, *Grace and Personality*, 156–57.

presented to each of us by ultimate reality itself as soon and as long as we exist humanly at all."[12]

DECISIVE RE-PRESENTATION

What does it mean to say that Jesus' re-presentation of God is *decisive*? As I've indicated, it means two things: clarity and challenge. First, it means that the teachings of Jesus clarify the character of God and the meaning of human existence so sharply that I literally recognize the reality of God that has made my life possible and that gives it everlasting meaning. Things snap into focus. My life makes sense in a way that it never has before. This leads to the second point. Jesus' revelation is decisive in the sense that it challenges me and demands a response from me; it forces me to choose for or against this way of understanding myself. I must either accept and live in accord with the truth or try to evade or deny it. I cannot be neutral. Not choosing is the same as choosing against. Jesus shows us how to understand ourselves rightly and calls us to become who we are.

RE-PRESENTATION AND ACTUALIZATION

The proclamation of Jesus is decisive *formally*, so to speak, because it forces a decision in the hearer. But what is it, *materially*, that makes the proclamation decisive? What is it about Jesus' message or his actions that justifies calling him "the Christ"? What is the criterion for our accepting the proclamation of Jesus as true?

An important point in Schubert Ogden's christology, which has always struck me as correct, is that Jesus is decisive because of the self-understanding he *re-presents* to us, not because of the self-understanding that he *realized*. The authority of Jesus' message does not depend upon whether or not he himself actualized it. Expressed otherwise, Jesus re-presents, but does not constitute, our salvation. God saves us, and Jesus proclaims it. This may seem shocking or even scandalous to some people, but it follows directly from the New Testament sources themselves.

12. Ogden, *Notebooks*, #472.

Unless we simply assume that the books of the New Testament were directly dictated by God as a kind of divine autobiography, we need to regard them as accounts *about* Jesus written by human beings. This means that the most we can recover from the texts is the authors' understanding of Jesus' self-understanding, rather than Jesus' own self-understanding itself. We have no direct access to what Jesus believed in his heart of hearts.

Furthermore, the authors of the New Testament were not eyewitnesses to the life and ministry of Jesus. The epistles of Paul were written around 50 AD, and the gospels between 70–100 AD. This means that the Jesus who is presented in the New Testament writings is a reconstruction based on memories and stories. The Gospels are theological *interpretations* of the significance of Jesus, rather than eyewitness historical accounts of his ministry. The Jesus of the New Testament is not simply the historical Jesus, but already the Jesus of faith. The Gospels are more concerned with the significance of Jesus' life than with its historical details. In the words of the New Testament theologian Willi Marxsen, "the intention was not to report, but to proclaim."[13]

But it's not just its inaccessibility that makes Jesus' own self-understanding an inappropriate criterion for his decisiveness. There is a theological reason, as well. Jesus taught that God's love is unearned, gratuitous, unconditional, and that our response to it must be unconditional, too. If, in order for us to trust entirely in God's love, we require proof that Jesus trusted it, aren't we putting a condition on our response to God? How is this different from saying that I will believe in God *if* my belly is full or *if* my life turns out well or *if* my country wins the war? If the teaching of Jesus confronts us with the gift of God's universal love and the demand that we live accordingly, then shouldn't we live accordingly *even if we were to discover that Jesus himself did not actually believe what he preached?* Does truth depend upon someone—even Jesus—believing it? Does a right way of living depend upon someone else having actualized it?

---

13. Marxsen, *Jesus and the Church*, 77.

Despite the inaccessibility of Jesus' own self-understanding, there is absolutely no reason to think that Jesus did not believe what he taught, and every reason to suppose that he did. Otherwise, the earliest witnesses would likely have dismissed him as a charlatan. The fundamental issue for me is not whether Jesus' life conformed to his proclamation, but why his proclamation is decisive *for me*? This brings us to the heart of the matter.

I am not asking why people do or do not believe in Jesus; I am asking why Jesus (more properly: his teachings and actions that are recoverable from our earliest sources) is believable? Why *should* we believe him? The sheer fact of its proclamation cannot be what makes something true. Otherwise, we should extend that privilege to any prophet whatsoever. Jim Jones in Guyana and David Koresh in Waco made proclamations to their followers, twisted and false proclamations, as it turns out. No, what makes a proclamation true is that it is, well, *true*. This means that there must be some independent criterion of its truth. What makes Jesus' message true is not that he proclaimed it or even that he believed it, but that it explains human experience—my experience—completely, so that I now see clearly what I've always dimly understood but actively resisted. In Ogden's words, Jesus' message can be validated only if "it answers one's underlying existential question about the meaning of one's existence more adequately than any alternative answer."[14]

At this point I want to pause and recall a moment in a graduate course on christology that I was teaching years ago. I was discussing—as I have been here—the question of what makes Jesus decisive for Christians, whether it is his message or his own self-understanding, when a student with a furrowed brow raised her hand and said: "Isn't it all just about God-made-man?" In other words, she was challenging my entire line of inquiry, because we know that Jesus is divine, and that is the source of his decisive authority. Period.

14. Ogden, *Notebooks*, #523.

DECISIVENESS AND DIVINITY

What, then, shall we say about the divinity of Jesus? The first thing is to point out that it is an assertion and, as I have argued several times above, an assertion is not true just because someone makes it or believes it. We need to look further.

Actually, the official teaching about the divinity of Jesus was debated and worked out over several hundred years in the early Church, culminating in the Council of Chalcedon in 451. The Council argued that its metaphysical expression ("two natures in one person") was an implication of the New Testament claims about Jesus, including that he was "the Christ," the "Son of Man," and the "Son of God," that he worked miracles, was born of a virgin, was raised from the dead, and so forth.

Here the work of the German theologian Rudolf Bultmann is important. The New Testament writings are religious documents that include both historical facts and mythological expressions. I am using "myth" here in the sense that Bultmann used it, as "the cosmology of a prescientific age."[15] The purpose of myth, Bultmann argues, is not to present an objective view of the world, but rather to express the sense of mystery or transcendence—to express the "other-worldly"—in terms that are derived from this world. So, for example, "divine transcendence is expressed as spatial distance;" God is "up there" or "out there."[16]

In dealing with mythological language, the two temptations are either to regard it as making historical claims that are literally true (for example, that creation happened over seven days) or to dismiss it as pure fancy, the naïve thinking of primitive peoples who lived before the scientific revolution. Both are mistakes. As Reinhold Niebuhr says, myths are to be taken "seriously, but not literally." What we should do is interpret what the myths are trying to tell us; that is, express the truth contained in the myths in non-mythological language, a project that Bultmann calls "demythologizing." So, for example, we might say that a creation story—whether expressed in terms of a cosmic egg or a world tree or a

15. Bultmann, *Kerygma and Myth*, 3.
16. Bultmann, *Kerygma and Myth*, 10, note 2.

Garden of Eden—articulates the human conviction that the meaning of the world lies beyond it.

Distinguishing what is historical and what is mythological in the New Testament is not simple. That there was an itinerant Jewish preacher, Jesus of Nazareth, who was executed by Roman authorities we know from historical sources outside the New Testament. But what about the miracle stories? Did Jesus heal people? Did he feed five thousand followers with a few loaves and fishes? And what about the resurrection story? Did the New Testament writers intend this to be understood as a physical resuscitation and an historical event, or were they using mythic categories to express their faith in the meaning of Jesus' life; their conviction that his teachings were true, despite his execution; and that they should live their lives according to them?

In answering this question as honestly as possible, it has been important to me to understand that some of the things the New Testament says about Jesus are not unlike claims made about other religious heroes in the religious literature of the era. Joshua J. Mark, for example, writes: "There is also the repetition of the figure known as the Dying and Reviving God, often a powerful entity himself, who is killed or dies and comes back to life for the good of his people: Osiris in Egypt, Krishna in India, the Maize God in Mesoamerica, Bacchus in Rome, Attis in Greece, Tammuz in Mesopotamia."[17] It turns out that miracle stories, even resurrections and ascensions, are common forms of religious discourse at the time of Jesus.

This leads me to a question: Are these titles and attributions (Son of God, virgin birth, resurrection, divine nature) literal or historical claims that *legitimize* Jesus' authority, or are they literary forms that are appropriated to *express* his authority? So far as I can tell, they are the latter: The attributions are at the service of "decisive," rather than vice versa.

Since it was not uncommon in religious literature at the time of the New Testament to attribute miracles and resurrections and ascensions to religious figures, the important thing is not so much *what* is said about Jesus, but rather that it is said *about Jesus*. It is

17. Mark, "Religion in the Ancient World."

because the teachings of Jesus had such existential power for his
followers that the New Testament authors use miracle stories and
titles to express his significance. And the fact that the metaphysical
divinity of Jesus was not claimed until 400 years later, after Christianity had moved out into the Greek world and appropriated its
philosophical concepts, seems to me to confirm this point: Divine
because decisive, not decisive because divine.

This means that questions such as: Did Jesus work miracles?
Was he resurrected? Was he divine?—interesting though they
are—are not the right questions to ask. Religiously speaking, the
important question is not Who is or was Jesus?, but rather Who is
the God that Jesus reveals? What is the authentic way to understand
myself that Jesus challenges me to accept?

This point is consistent with the earliest Christian witness
that we can recover, what Willi Marxsen calls the "Jesus-kerygma,"
the proclamation concerning Jesus by his followers, even before the crucifixion. What is striking about Marxsen's research is
his conclusion that "this kerygma does not call for faith *in* Jesus
Christ. . .people allowed themselves to be moved by him, and in
this being moved, they believed *him*, without formulating this as
belief *in* him."[18] Or, as Ogden makes the point: "Thus, while the
earliest stratum of witness is very definitely witness to Jesus, it is
a witness to him in which he himself appears as a witness—not to
himself but to the imminent coming of the rule of God, and to its
gift and demand already present in his own witness."[19] What the
earliest community took to be decisive about Jesus was what *God*
was doing through him.

Among the various titles attributed to Jesus, one in particular
helps to make this point: Jesus is the Word of God. The function
of words is to express thoughts, to say what is in someone's mind.
When I listen to a speaker, the more I concentrate on the words
themselves—the way they are accented or inflected—the more I am
distracted from what the words are trying to convey. The words get
in the way of the message. Thinking of Jesus as the "window" of

18. Marxsen, *Jesus and the Church*, 88–89.
19. Ogden, *Notebooks*, #521.

God makes the same point. The purpose of a window is to reveal the landscape, and the more transparent it is, the less it is noticed, the better is its revelation. Conversely, the more we focus on the window itself, its thickness or a reflection in it, the more we are distracted from the landscape.

In short, when the divinization of Jesus—or his pre-existence or virgin birth or resurrection—becomes the point, rather than an expression of the theistic point, we run the risk of distraction and even of idolatry.

What, then, is the criterion of Jesus' decisiveness, if not divinity? It can only be the clarifying power of his message coupled with its confrontational challenge. Jesus is decisive because in his teaching I re-cognize the truth about human existence—about my life—when I am confronted by it so clearly. Through Jesus my existential faith in life's meaning is lifted up to the conscious level, and I am challenged to live accordingly. All will be well because I am a beloved child of God. Go and love likewise.

4

Action

FROM WHETHER AND WHY TO HOW?

WE BEGAN WITH THE question of suicide—whether life is worth living. The answer is yes. We always live, even if unconsciously, by a confidence that our lives have abiding meaning. So, the deeper question is not *whether*, but *why* life is meaningful? What is it that calls forth our basic confidence? The answer is that the universe is benevolent, that our environment is theistic, that the ground of our being is both supremely sensitive and supremely stable. Jesus preaches what good philosophy teaches: that God is love. What, then, must we do? How ought we to live?

LIVING REALISTICALLY

The quick and simple answer is: *We ought to live according to what is real, rather than at cross-purposes to it.* "Living realistically" doesn't mean that we should conform our lives to just any particular social order, and especially not to any of the terrible "isms"—racism, sexism, totalitarianism, and so forth that continue to haunt our world. Living realistically does not mean resignation to injustice. It means, rather, living according to the way reality is structured, if not necessarily to the way a society is organized. Living realistically means living according to what is metaphysically or ontologically *true* and using that truth to guide our personal, social, and political efforts. If, for example, the truth is that reality is social and its highest expression is love, then any life plan that is based on *me-first* or *zero-sum* or *dog-eat-dog* is working against the grain of what is actually true.

One of the great themes in Greek thought is that human happiness consists of living our lives according to what is true. For the Greeks, happiness is not so much an emotion or a feeling as it is the right relationship between the way we live and the way things are. Unhappiness, conversely, means living out of harmony with what is true. Expressing this in modern terms, we can say that human happiness means living authentically, and unhappiness means living inauthentically, where "authentic" means "consistent with what is true" or "synchronized with the truth." Happiness means living realistically "without illusion or lies."[1]

An analogy may be found in the area of physical health. Every time we begin a diet or exercise program we illustrate the point that our well-being requires that we live in conformity with certain basic truths: Not too much fat or sugar or salt; lots of vegetables and fruit and fiber. Happiness, like health, requires us to live according to what is true.

The Greeks identified fundamental laws of nature which, when we violate them, lead to disaster, and when we live in accord with them, lead to happiness. I am not talking about physical laws such as gravity—though ignoring gravity will definitely lead to unhappiness!—but laws about human nature having to do with right relationships and right actions. This is a key to understanding Greek tragedy. Consider, for example, the story of Oedipus. He killed a stranger he did not know was actually his father, and he fell in love with and married a woman he did not know was really his mother. Patricide and incest are actions against nature; in committing them, Oedipus crossed the line, he lived out of harmony with the truth, and the result was tragedy. Once the truth was revealed, Oedipus' mother Jocasta killed herself and Oedipus blinded himself

---

1. Comte-Sponville, *The Little Book of Philosophy*, Kindle loc. 88.

and went into exile. Oedipus forfeited happiness because he did not know what was true.

The American sociologist of religion, Clifford Geertz, has argued that this Greek insight about the connection between worldview and lifestyle, between what we understand to be true and how we ought to live, has wide application across human cultures. He writes, for example, about the different lifestyles of Navaho Indians, French people, and Hindus and shows how their different ethics are grounded in their different interpretations of the world. Although they disagree about what they think is true, they all agree that how we ought to live is authorized by what we understand to be true. "Ought" comes from "is."[2]

If human happiness is indeed an alignment between how we live and what is true, then—obviously—we need to know what is true. Oedipus *did not know what was really true*, but his ignorance did not absolve him from tragic consequences. Crossing the line out of ignorance rather than malice is still crossing the line. We need to be able to separate falsehood from truth, appearance from reality. What is true—and what is only an illusion? I remember the poignant story of an elderly man who had lived through the end of Soviet rule in Latvia. Almost overnight, the country moved from a centralized Soviet ideology to a decentralized democratic worldview. The old man confessed to a friend of mine that he no longer knew what was true. "All my life I've been told how the world is, and now they say it is otherwise. I don't know what to believe anymore." How can a person who is so profoundly disoriented and deeply confused ever be said to be happy in any significant sense?

In a world where truth is politicized, where disinformation and lying abound, where marketing is powerful and seductive, we must work especially hard to find out what is true. For decades in America, tobacco companies, through sophisticated advertising, were able to portray cigarette smoking as glamorous for women and as rugged and sexy for men. I myself was drawn into this illusion for years. I remember looking at a package of cigarettes in

2. Geertz, *The Interpretation of Cultures*, 126–31.

Canada once. On the side of the package was a warning: Cigarettes can kill you. That was the truth. I changed my lifestyle.

WHAT IS TRUE?

Reality as Social Process, the title of one of Hartshorne's books, conveys succinctly a general view of existence that has been carefully worked out by Whitehead and Hartshorne in their neoclassical philosophy. To be is to be in relation to others; to be is to be *from*, *in* and *for* community. We are born into a world that we inherit from others; we depend upon others to help us while we live; and we exit, having enhanced or diminished the world for those coming after us. In the words of Martin Luther King, Jr., "We are tied together in the single garment of destiny, caught in an inescapable network of mutuality. . .This is the way God's universe is made; this is the way it is structured."

We say correctly that "no person is an island." Even the independent "self-made" person is not entirely independent or self-made at all. That person did not raise himself, did not construct the language or arithmetic that he uses daily, did not build the roads or the airports that he depends upon, did not create the healthcare or educational systems that allow him to prosper. We all need others. All our experiences are intrinsically social. Even in extreme isolation we are related to our bodies, our thoughts, our memories. We are in society the way a fish is in water.

We have first-hand experience of the social structure of reality literally every moment. Our lives are a constant stream of momentary experiences, hundreds if not thousands each day. Each experience has the same social structure: subjects interacting with others. Right now, you are reacting to my words and thoughts, and also to whatever else is going on in your environment, including bodily feelings (tired? hungry? worried? too warm?) and the activity of others (child in the room? someone texting you? wondering about a co-worker?). This list could be expanded to include all the activities of your own past—habits you have developed, for example—as well as the past activities of others that have had an impact on you.

The point is that an individual life is made up of experiences that are intrinsically relational.

The fact that I am inescapably dependent on others does not mean that my relationships entirely define me. Built into the social structure of reality is a measure of freedom, self-determination, creativity. Reality is not like a giant billiards game where objects act and react predictably according to strict laws (even subatomic particles have a degree of unpredictability). In any given moment I am reacting to my past and interacting with my neighbors, but *how* I react, the *way* I deal with my surroundings, is up to me. It is a matter of choice. I will take care for this. I will ignore that. I will continue to nurse my grudge. I will begin to let go and forgive. And so forth.

Experience is social not only in the broad sense that we relate to those around us, but also in the dynamic sense that our relations invite or provoke further interaction. The social structure of reality is self-perpetuating. You and I are having a conversation. I speak and you react, and then I react to your reaction, and then you react to my reaction to your reaction. Experience is always experience of other experience. Experience yields experience.

There is thus a rhythmic pulse, a back-and-forth, to reality: taking and giving, receiving and offering, inheriting and bequeathing. Whitehead expressed this in a memorable phrase: "The many become one and are increased by one."[3] That is, the many people and things in my field of attention are gathered together in my momentary experience, and my integrated reaction then becomes a new datum for others—including future versions of myself—to experience.

The social character of reality provides the criterion for how we should live. If reality is social, then we should act in ways that promote community and enhance relations. Here is how Charles Hartshorne puts it: "To be social is to weave one's own life out of strands taken from the lives of others and to furnish one's own life

---

3. Whitehead, *Process and Reality*, 26.

as a strand to be woven into their lives."[4] Contributionism—what others offer us and what we offer to others—is the DNA of life.

Whitehead observed that God should be conceived, not as the great exception to, but rather as the chief exemplification of, this general view of existence. Indeed, one of the most attractive features of neoclassical theism is that it provides a powerful philosophical expression of the New Testament claim that God is love. To believe in God is, Andre Comte-Sponville points out, "to believe that this supreme value (love) is also the supreme truth (God)."[5]

Reality is social and its highest expression is love: This is what is true. "Living realistically" thus means living according to love. As Niebuhr puts it: "The law of love is really the law of life. It is a basic requirement of human existence which men transgress at their peril."[6] We come from love and we return to love. Along the way we are to love one another.

THE MEANING OF LOVE

What does "love" mean? The word is used so often—especially in contemporary America, where everybody from celebrities to performers to politicians professes to love nearly everybody else—that it has become vague and stretched thin. Attraction, admiration, preference, well-wishing, enjoyment, desire, commitment—all of these and more are potential meanings of "I love you." How can we get our arms around something so broad? What are we really talking about?

As usual, the reflections of the ancient Greeks are helpful starting points. They distinguished two types of human love: eros and philia. Although we often identify the erotic with sexuality, the essence of eros is not sex; it is possessiveness, and sexuality is a particularly powerful way of expressing it. Eros is the desire for something or some person that we do not have. I need that car; I want that man or that woman. Eros is based on the absence of

4. Hartshorne, *Reality as Social Process*, 136.

5. Comte-Sponville, *Little Book on Philosophy*, Kindle loc. 969.

6. Davis and Good, *Reinhold Niebuhr on Politics*, 134.

what we want; it is the desire to have, to possess, to control. Eros is a covetous love, loving the other for one's own sake. In that sense, it is really an extension of the ego, of the self. When I actually have what I had lacked, the flame of passion dies out, and so purely erotic relationships usually wither sooner or later.

Philia is a different and higher form of human love. Philia is a generous or benevolent love; it is love of the other for the other's own sake. Philia is based not on desire for what is absent, but on celebration of what is present. Philia is joyful, and it does not seek to possess or control. Philia says: I like who you are; I enjoy your presence; the world is better with you in it. Philia is usually translated as the love of friends, but it is "friends" in a deep and broad sense. Aristotle included the love of parents for their children and for each other, the love of siblings, the love of lovers, and the love of friends in the scope of philia.

Eros and philia are ideal types. They show us that love has two dimensions, what I call passion and action. As we move from eros to philia, passion evolves from covetous desire to empathetic response (feeling the feelings of the beloved), and action evolves from possessiveness to beneficence (acting for the good of the beloved).

Eros and philia are often mixed together. Passion attracts, and appreciation sustains. Long-term lovers respect one another, even as they desire one another; they give each other needed space and independence, and do not demand as the price of admission that the other make them happy. They support and console each other, and act on behalf of—for the benefit of—the beloved.

Human love is finite. We are capable of sustaining only a few deep friendships in our lives, partly because of the time and emotional energy required, but also because an element of self-love remains even in our love of friends. We love those who love us. Perhaps we do not love them only *because* they love us, but still we do not befriend those who are indifferent or hostile to us. "Self-love both makes friendship possible and restricts its scope."[7]

Our circle of friends is limited, but still we have moral obligations and responsibilities to people outside the zone of our love.

7. Comte-Sponville, *A Small Treatise on the Great Virtues*, 268.

Generally speaking, these obligations fall into two categories: nega-tive (do no harm; respect others' rights), and positive (help other people; do the greatest good for the greatest number). The relative weight to be assigned to each category is a subject of debate among moral philosophers. Have I discharged my obligation to others if I leave them alone and do them no harm, or must I do more and actually work to increase their well-being? For the sake of helping many, can I violate the rights of a few? And what about those who seek to harm me? Do I—or my country—have any moral obliga-tions toward an enemy? These are complex issues that do not have simple answers, and I do not intend to pursue them further here. My point is that although human love is limited, moral obligation is broader. Morality is necessary because love is lacking. If we all loved one another, moral rules would not be necessary, because we would always act in the interest of everyone else, each of whom would be considered our beloved.

So far, so good. We seem to have a general roadmap for living realistically, and so living well. The secret of life is to move beyond possessiveness (which ultimately frustrates us anyway) to respect, empathy, and beneficence for those we love, and to observe our ethical obligations toward all the others.

GIFT AND DEMAND: AGAPIC LOVE AND OUR IMPOSSIBLE POSSIBILITY

And then along comes Jesus the teacher who redraws the map. You love your friends who love you back? How praiseworthy is that? Rather, you should love your neighbor—*all* your neighbors—as yourself. Your attitude toward this hungry street person here and now or this particular Syrian refugee or this grieving mother who has lost her son in a tragic confrontation with police—your attitude toward these neighbors should be the same as your own self-regard. Do not just respect and do no harm to these people, but actually *love* them, which is to say: feel their misery and do something to relieve it, just as you would for yourself or your children or your closest friends. If someone—anyone—needs your shirt, give them your coat as well. If someone is hostile and hits you, turn your other cheek. Forgive seventy times seven. Love your enemies; *do good to those who would harm you.*

What is this? How can I possibly act on behalf of all who are suffering around me, much less around the globe? And what sense could it conceivably make for me to love those who are mean or vicious or evil? Do good to Hitler? Love a jihadist who would murder the innocent? Really? Really? It is shocking how shocking Jesus' teachings are—and how little we Christians are shocked by them. As Reinhold Niebuhr remarked: "The modern pulpit would be saved from much sentimentality if the thousands of sermons which are annually preached upon these texts would contain some suggestions of the impossibility of these ethical demands. . ."[8]

What are we to make of the fact that the ethical teachings of Jesus are impossible for us to realize? Why would we even try to follow them?

To answer this question, we need to understand that the love that Jesus preaches is not eros or philia; it is agape. "God is love" means "God is *agape*." The Greek word *agape* is translated into Latin as *caritas* and into English as "charity." It does not mean almsgiving or tithing or out-of-pocket donations to homeless people. Agape is love that is universal and indiscriminate. Agape is the way God loves us. Jesus tells us that our heavenly father makes the sun rise on the good and the bad alike and sends the rain on the honest and the dishonest. The laborer who arrives at the eleventh hour is paid the same wage as the one who showed up at dawn. Agape is entirely gratuitous and unearned; love that does not wait to be deserved. Jesus preaches that God loves us, even though we are sinners. We do not earn or merit divine agape. In this sense, divine agape is entirely creative. Agapic love does not originate as a response to value; it creates value. We are not loved because we are lovable; we are lovable because we are first loved.

The closest human approximation to unconditional love is parental love, and especially maternal love at its best. Mothers and fathers love their children even before they know them. In the best

---

8. Niebuhr, *An Interpretation of Christian Ethics*, 28.

cases, children are carried in the womb of someone who already loves them, and they are born into an atmosphere of love that they have not earned. Children learn to love others because they have first been loved. As one philosopher put it: "all love begins as something received and only later is something we learn to give. . ... the grace of being loved precedes the grace of loving and prepares us for it."[9]

The ethic of Jesus is rooted in thankful recognition of the agapic love that has rescued us from insignificance and made our lives worthwhile. We want to imitate agapic love because we want to be true to the pure unbounded love that has been shown us. Like an elderly couple whose love for one another includes a faithfulness to their earlier, younger love, we children of God ought to love others out of gratitude for God's love of us. As Willi Marxsen has put it memorably: The believer "personally acts in God's place toward his or her neighbor."[10]

The sole reference point for the ethic of Jesus is thus vertical; it is centered on the sovereignty of divine love. People are lovable, not because of anything they have done or not done to us, but just because God loves them. Precious to God, therefore precious to me—this is the simple logic of a theocentric ethics.

But can we even imagine a world in which each of us loves *everyone* the way a good mother loves her children? Can we imagine ever fulfilling Jesus' counsel to "Be perfect, even as your heavenly Father is perfect"? Of what possible practical use is such an obviously impossible ideal? The answer is twofold.

First of all, precisely as an ideal, agape can orient our lives, give them direction, give us something to aim for. Even if it always exceeds our grasp, the agapic ideal can extend our reach. It can arouse us from complacency, wake us from our moral slumber. For example, agape forces us to confront human misery, to feel it, to act to relieve it.

A widespread problem facing humanity is the unfair disparity between haves and have-nots, between rich and poor, between

---

9. Comte-Sponville, *A Small Treatise on the Great Virtues*, 261.

10. Marxsen, *Jesus and the Church*, 75.

winners and losers. Sometimes, but not that often really, the gulf between winners and losers can be explained entirely in terms of personal effort or personal laziness. But much of the time, the huge difference between the haves and the have-nots is the result of sheer (good or bad) luck: Where you are born, when you are born, to whom you are born. Those of us who are the winners often forget how much of our good fortune is an accident. As the saying goes: He woke up on third base and decided he had hit a triple.

Life is deeply unfair. When I was in Tanzania, I held a toddler orphan who was so desperate for touch and attention that he wailed inconsolably every time I put him down. When I was a boy, my father read poetry to me and told me that he loved me. What different life arcs were already launched for little-Larry and the African orphan.

In addition to luck, the gulf between haves and have-nots is a matter of deliberate effort by the winners to guarantee that they stay on top. Racism in America, for example, is structural, institutionalized inequality. Racism is designed, in the words of a recent book, to enforce a caste system of winners and losers in America. In much the same way that history is written by the winners, American society—its laws, the way it works, its rules about who gets to do what—was designed by the continental victors, and not by the slaves or the native peoples—or the women, for that matter.

The gap is not only unfair and unfortunate, it is dangerous. What must life be like at the bottom of the heap where you have literally nothing to lose? The rage of young Palestinians gives us a clue. How desperate does a sixteen-year-old girl have to be to detonate her suicide vest? If I imagine myself living in the losers' world, I have to admit that I, too, would be furious at my lot, and maybe even violent. Much of the pain in the world results from this problem of haves and have-nots, and until we face it, name it, and address it, the ills will persist and fester. Because the problem is systemic rather than incidental ("just a few bad apples"), any realistic solution will have to be structural rather than voluntary ("a thousand points of light"), a matter of justice and not just of charity. Agape has political implications.

Agape is a blunt reminder that it is easier for us to reflect theologically about the problem of evil than to face the horror. I remember visiting the Holocaust museum in Washington, D.C. and looking at film footage (shown behind a modest wall to prevent children from seeing) of naked, confused, scared humans being herded into gas chambers. I thought, "I should not watch this; I am a voyeur." Then I thought, "Watch this. Let it hurt. Let it disturb your life and haunt your sleep. *You owe it to them*."

In addition to motivating us, the agapic ideal stands in judgement of us—and this is its second function. It is both the power in our actions and the power over against our actions. Agape is a bright beacon that beckons us, but it also shines an unwelcome light on our secrets and the dark corners we don't want revealed. It reminds us that self-interest shadows all our actions, tainting even our highest accomplishments and achievements. Tax reformers will not raise their own rates; health care legislators are unlikely to purchase plans they craft for others; redistricting efforts will surely benefit the party in control. I give a passionate talk about the ills of racism and am a bit proud and puffed-up if it is well-received. I give a major gift to a good cause and enjoy seeing my name toward the top of the donor list. Good actions all, headed in the right direction, but always sneaking self-protection and self-promotion into the deal.

The agapic ideal reminds us that we humans (and our nation) are all "mixed bags," curious combinations of noble and ignoble acts and motives, public and private personae, things of which we can be proud and things of which we should be ashamed. If we were all fully transparent to ourselves and to one another—morally naked, so to speak—we would likely forgive the sins of others because we—and they—see the sin in ourselves. Our attitude toward ourselves and the world would be mercy. We are all damaged goods. This, I think, is an essential interpretive key in the "love your enemies" command. The evil in the foe is also in the self.

As Reinhold Niebuhr has argued, in all human affairs the possibilities for evil grow together with the possibilities for good. Social media platforms which hold the promise of uniting humanity and offering global access to information have also devolved into extremely effective instruments of disinformation and hate. The good and the evil come packaged together in our fallen world. Agape calls this out.

Trying to live according to the ethic of Jesus thus means living with tension and paradox. It means trying and failing, getting up and trying again. We are ever and again to act on behalf of our neighbor—including the enemy and especially the vulnerable, even though we are imperfect, and all our achievements will likely be stained with self-interest. This radical ideal—what Niebuhr calls "history's impossible possibility"—that we should strive to imitate divine agape, that we should actually try to love *all* our neighbors, even those who do not deserve to be loved *and even though we will fail*— "this dumb, blind love is man's meaning."[11]

Agape helps us understand the Great Commandment: Love God with your whole heart, and your neighbor as yourself. But how can we love God with our *whole* heart, and still have some heart left for the neighbor, unless loving God *is* loving the neighbor, and loving the neighbor *is* loving God? This is the great and powerful message of Christian theism. It is the point also made in the Gospel narrative of the Last Judgement: What you do to the least of these—the hungry, the bereaved, the imprisoned—you do to God.

This scene also makes clear that, in the end, "right" beliefs and "right" understandings, as helpful as they are in our lives, are not the point of our lives. Our beliefs, our philosophies, will not save us. The point is love. The point is how we take care of one another and other sentient life, what we make possible for our descendants, how we preserve mother planet, how we enrich the divine experience. Charity alone survives. Love is our origin, our purpose, our end, our commandment.

Walt Whitman's poem, "The Base of All Metaphysics," will serve as an apt summary of this essay, this record of what I have learned about life's meaning.

---

11. Grossman, *Life and Fate*, 410.

TESTAMENT

AND now, gentlemen,
A word I give to remain in your memories and minds,
As base, and finale too, for all metaphysics.

(So, to the students, the old professor,
At the close of his crowded course.)   5

Having studied the new and antique, the Greek and Germanic
systems,
Kant having studied and stated—Fichte and Schelling and Hegel,
Stated the lore of Plato—and Socrates, greater than Plato,
And greater than Socrates sought and stated—Christ divine having
studied long,
I see reminiscent to-day those Greek and Germanic systems,   10
See the philosophies all—Christian churches and tenets see,
Yet underneath Socrates clearly see—and underneath Christ the
divine I see,
The dear love of man for his comrade—the attraction of friend to
friend,
Of the well-married husband and wife—of children and parents,
Of city for city, and land for land.   15

To Whitman's wonderful words I would add only that the
"dear love" of which he speaks is also our grateful love of God, our
contribution to the everlasting tapestry being woven.

Bibliography

Bair, Deirdre. *Samuel Beckett*. New York: Harcourt Brace Jovanovich, 1978.

Berger, Peter. *A Rumor of Angels: Modern Society and the Rediscovery of the Supernatural*. Garden City, NY: Doubleday, 1969.

Bultmann, Rudolf, et al. *Kerygma and Myth*. New York: Harper and Row, 1961.

Camus, Albert. *The Myth of Sisyphus and Other Essays*. Translated by Justin O'Brien. New York: Random House, 1955.

———. "The Riddle." *Atlantic Monthly*. June 1986, 83–85.

Comte-Sponville, Andre, *The Little Book of Philosophy*. Translated by Frank Wynne. London: Vintage Books, 2005. Kindle edition.

———. *A Small Treatise on the Great Virtues*. Metropolitan Books, 2002. Kindle edition.

Davis, Harry R. and Good, Robert C., eds. *Reinhold Niebuhr on Politics*. New York: Charles Scribner's Sons, 1960.

Freud, Sigmund. *The Future of an Illusion*. Translated by W.D. Robson-Scott. Garden City, NY: Doubleday & Company, 1964.

Gamwell, Franklin I. *Existence and the Good: Metaphysical Necessity in Morals and Politics*. Albany, NY: SUNY Press, 2011.

Geertz, Clifford. *The Interpretation of Cultures*. New York: Basic Books, 1973.

Grossman, Vasily. *Life and Fate*. Translated by Robert Chandler. New York; NYRB Classics, 2006.

Hartshorne, Charles. *The Divine Relativity: A Social Conception of God*. New Haven and London: Yale University Press, 1948.

———. *Man's Vision of God and the Logic of Theism*. Chicago: Willett, Clark & Co., 1941; reprint ed., Hamden, CT: Archon Books, 1964.

———. *A Natural Theology for Our Time*. LaSalle, IL: Open Court, 1967.

———. *Reality as Social Process: Studies in Metaphysics and Religion*. Glencoe, IL: Free Press, 1953; reprint ed., New York: Hafner Publishing Co., 1971.

Küng, Hans. *Does God Exist? An Answer for Today*. Translated by Edward Quinn. Garden City, NY: Doubleday & Company, Inc., 1980.

Leclerc, Ivor. *Whitehead's Metaphysics*. New Jersey: Humanities Press, 1978.

Mark, Joshua J.. "Religion in the Ancient World." *World History Encyclopedia*. Last modified March 23, 2018. https://www.worldhistory.org/religion/.

Marxsen, Willi. *Jesus and the Church: The Beginnings of Christianity*. Translated by Philip E. Devenish. Philadelphia: Trinity Press International, 1992.

Niebuhr, Reinhold. *Christianity and Power Politics*. New York: Charles Scribner's Sons, 1946.

———. *An Interpretation of Christian Ethics*. New York: Seabury, 1979.

Nussbaum, Martha C. *Upheavals of Thought: The Intelligence of Emotions*. Cambridge: Cambridge University Press, 2003.

Ogden, Schubert M. *Christ Without Myth*. New York: Harper & Row, 1961.

———. *A Colloquium on The Credibility of 'God.'* New Concord, OH: Muskingum College, 1967.

———. *The Reality of God*. New York: Harper & Row, 1963.

———. *The Schubert M. Ogden Notebooks*. http://bit.ly/OgdenNotebooks.

———. "Theology and Religious Studies: Their Difference and the Difference It Makes." *Journal of the American Academy of Religion*, March 1978, 3–17.

Oman, John. *Grace and Personality*. Cambridge: Cambridge University Press, 1919.

Tracy, David. *Blessed Rage for Order: The New Pluralism in Theology*. New York: Seabury Press, 1975.

Whitehead, Alfred North. *Modes of Thought*. New York: The Free Press, 1968.

———. *Process and Reality*. New York: The Free Press, 1969

———. *Science and the Modern World*. New York: The Free Press, 1967.

———. *Symbolism: Its Meaning and Effect*. New York: Capricorn Books, 1959.

Made in the USA
Middletown, DE
21 August 2024